The ESSENTIALS® of

REGISTERED TRADEMARK

UNITED STATES HISTORY

1912 to 1941
World War I, the Depression
and the New Deal

William Turner, Ph.D.
Professor of History
Pembroke State University
Pembroke, North Carolina

D1114254

Research and Education Association
61 Ethel Road West
Piscataway, New Jersey 08854

THE ESSENTIALS®
OF UNITED STATES HISTORY
1912 to 1941
World War I, the Depression,
and the New Deal

Printed in the United States of America

Library of Congress Catalog Card Number 94-74859

International Standard Book Number 0-87891-716-0

ESSENTIALS is a registered trademark of
Research & Education Association, Piscataway, New Jersey 08854

What the "Essentials of History" Will Do for You

REA's "Essentials of History" series offers a new approach to the study of history that is different from what has been available previously. Each book in the series has been designed to steer a sensible middle course, by including neither too much nor too little information.

Compared with conventional history outlines, the "Essentials of History" offer far more detail, with fuller explanations and interpretations of historical events and developments. Compared with voluminous historical tomes and textbooks, the "Essentials of History" offer a far more concise, less ponderous overview of each of the periods they cover.

The "Essentials of History" are intended primarily to aid students in studying history, doing homework, writing papers and preparing for exams. The books are organized to provide quick access to information and explanations of the important events, dates, and persons of the period. The books can be used in conjunction with any text. They will save hours of study and preparation time while providing a firm grasp and insightful understanding of the subject matter.

Instructors too will find the "Essentials of History" useful. The books can assist in reviewing or modifying course outlines. They also can assist with preparation of exams, as well as serve as an efficient memory refresher.

In sum, the "Essentials of History" will prove to be handy reference sources at all times.

The authors of the series are respected experts in their fields. They present clear, well-reasoned explanations and interpretations of the complex political, social, cultural, economic and philosophical issues and developments which characterize each era.

In preparing these books REA has made every effort to assure their accuracy and maximum usefulness. We are confident that each book will prove enjoyable and valuable to its user.

Dr. Max Fogiel, Program Director

About the Author

William P. Turner began his teaching career as an instructor at Fairmont State College in Fairmont, West Virginia in 1955. He then served Fairmont State from 1955 to 1978 as professor, chairman of the department of history and social science, dean of academic affairs, and vice president for administrative affairs and professor of history. He served as director of academic affairs and student services on the West Virginia Board of Regents from 1970 to 1974. Since 1978 he has served Pembroke State University in Pembroke, North Carolina as vice chancellor for academic affairs and as a professor of history.

Dr. Turner maintains memberships in the Southern Historical Association and the Association of Historians in North Carolina, and has authored histories on West Virginia dentistry, Fairmont State College, and the politician John T. McGraw. He is presently working in American social history.

CONTENTS

CHAPTER 1

WOODROW WILSON AND THE NEW FREEDOM

1.1 THE ELECTION OF 1912

1.1.1 *Political Divisions*

Both the Republicans and the Democrats were divided with conservative and progressive factions. Discontent with both parties turned many toward the Socialist Party.

1.1.2 *The Republicans*

The nomination was sought by incumbent President William Howard Taft, who had aligned himself with the Old Guard or conservative faction, and by former President Theodore Roosevelt, who had assumed the leadership of the Insurgent or progressive wing of the party. Roosevelt had won 278 of the 382 delegates to the national convention elected by primary elections, but Taft controlled the Republican National Committee and the party machinery. At the convention, the Taft-controlled Credentials Committee awarded most of the 254 seats challenged by Roosevelt to Taft, who won the nomination on

1

the first ballot. Roosevelt supporters abstained or walked out. The Republican platform was moderately progressive, but the Old Guard dominated the party.

1.1.3 *The Democrats*

The Democratic National Convention voted forty-six times before Woodrow Wilson, the reform governor of New Jersey, secured the necessary two-thirds vote for nomination. His principal opponent was the more conservative speaker of the House of Representatives, J. Beauchamp (Champ) Clark of Missouri. William Jennings Bryan threw the support of most of the old populist wing of the party to Wilson. Wilson's platform, called the New Freedom, proposed the elimination of special privileges for big interests by restoring competition through the breakup of monopolies. The checks and balances of the free enterprise system would then function automatically to protect the public interest. It also advocated lower tariffs and reform of the money and banking system.

1.1.4 *The Progressives*

Roosevelt supporters assembled in August after the regular conventions to form the Progressive or Bull Moose Party with Roosevelt as its presidential nominee. Roosevelt's platform, the New Nationalism, proposed that business monopolies be left intact and controlled or counterbalanced by government regulation in the public interest. He also endorsed federal old age, unemployment, and accident insurance; the eight-hour day; woman suffrage; the abolition of child labor; and expanded public health services.

1.1.5 *The Socialists*

Perennial candidate Eugene V. Debs was the nominee. The platform proposed a gradual transition to government ownership of major industries.

1.1.6 *The Election*

Wilson carried 41 states for 435 electoral votes with 6,286,000 popular votes, or 41.9 percent of the total. Roosevelt carried 6 states for 88 electoral votes with 4,126,000 popular votes. Taft carried 2 states for 8 electoral votes with 3,484,000 popular votes, and Debs polled a surprising 897,000 popular votes.

1.2 IMPLEMENTING THE NEW FREEDOM: THE EARLY YEARS OF THE WILSON ADMINISTRATION

1.2.1 *The New President*

Wilson was only the second Democrat (Cleveland was the first) elected president since the Civil War. He was born in Virginia in 1856, the son of a Presbyterian minister, and was reared and educated in the South. After earning a doctorate at Johns Hopkins University, he taught history and political science at Princeton, and in 1902 became president of that university. In 1910 he was elected governor of New Jersey as a reform or progressive Democrat.

1.2.2 *The Cabinet*

The key appointments were William Jennings Bryan as secretary of state and William Gibbs McAdoo as secretary of the treasury.

1.2.3 *The Inaugural Address*

Wilson called the Congress, now controlled by Democrats, into a special session beginning April 7, 1913 to consider three topics:

1) Reduction of the tariff.

2) Reform of the national banking and currency laws.

3) Improvements in the antitrust laws.

On April 8 he appeared personally before Congress, the first president since John Adams to do so, to promote his program.

1.2.4 The Underwood-Simmons Tariff Act of 1913

Average rates were reduced to about twenty-nine percent as compared with thirty-seven to forty percent under the previous Payne-Aldrich Tariff. A graduated income tax was included in the law to compensate for lost tariff revenue. It ranged from a tax of one percent on personal and corporate incomes over $4,000, a figure well above the annual income of the average worker, to seven percent on incomes over $500,000. The sixteenth amendment to the Constitution, ratified in February 1913, authorized the income tax.

1.2.5 The Federal Reserve Act of 1913

Background. Following the Panic of 1907, it was generally agreed that there was need for more stability in the banking industry and for a currency supply which would expand and contract to meet business needs. Three points of view on the subject developed:

1) Most Republicans backed the proposal of a commission headed by Senator Nelson W. Aldrich for a large central bank controlled by private banks.

2) Bryanite Democrats, pointing to the Wall Street influence exposed by the 1913 Pujo Committee investigation of the money trust, wanted a reserve system and

4

currency owned and controlled by the government.

3) Conservative Democrats favored a decentralized system privately owned and controlled but free from Wall Street.

The bill which finally passed in December 1913 was a compromise measure. Provisions of the law were as follows:

1) The nation was divided into twelve regions with a Federal Reserve bank in each region.

2) Commercial banks in the region owned the Federal Reserve Bank by purchasing stock equal to six percent of their capital and surplus, and elected the directors of the bank. National banks were required to join the system, and state banks were invited to join.

3) The Federal Reserve Banks held the gold reserves of their members.

4) Federal Reserve Banks loaned money to member banks by rediscounting their commercial and agricultural paper. That is, the money was loaned at interest less than the public paid to the member banks, and the notes of indebtedness of businesses and farmers to the member banks were held as collateral. This allowed the Federal Reserve to control interest rates by raising or lowering the discount rate.

5) The money loaned to the member banks was in the form of a new currency, Federal Reserve Notes, which was backed sixty percent by commercial paper and forty percent by gold. This currency was designed to expand and contract with the volume of business activity and borrowing.

6) Checks on member banks were cleared through the Federal Reserve System.

7) The Federal Reserve System serviced the financial needs of the federal government.

8) The system was supervised and policy was set by a national Federal Reserve Board composed of the secretary of the Treasury, the comptroller of the currency, and five other members appointed by the president of the United States.

1.2.6 *The Clayton Antitrust Act of 1914*

This law supplemented and interpreted the Sherman Antitrust Act of 1890. The principal provisions were as follows:

1) Stock ownership by a corporation in a competing corporation was prohibited.

2) Interlocking directorates of competing corporations were prohibited. That is, the same persons could not manage competing corporations.

3) Price discrimination (charging less in some regions than in others to undercut the competition) and exclusive contracts which reduced competition were prohibited.

4) Officers of corporations could be held personally responsible for violations of antitrust laws.

5) Labor unions and agricultural organizations were not to be considered "combinations or conspiracies in restraint of trade" as defined by the Sherman Antitrust Act.

1.2.7 The Federal Trade Commission Act of 1914

The law prohibited all unfair trade practices without defining them, and created a commission of five members appointed by the president. The commission was empowered to issue cease and desist orders to corporations to stop actions considered to be in restraint of trade, and to bring suit in the courts if the orders were not obeyed. Firms could also contest the orders in court. Under previous antitrust legislation, the government could act against corporations only by bringing suit.

1.2.8 Evaluation

The Underwood-Simmons Tariff, the Federal Reserve Act, and the Clayton Act were clearly in accord with the principles of the New Freedom, but the Federal Trade Commission reflected a move toward the kind of government regulation advocated by Roosevelt in his New Nationalism. Nonetheless, in 1914 and 1915 Wilson continued to oppose federal government action in such matters as loans to farmers, child labor regulation, and woman suffrage.

1.3 THE TRIUMPH OF NEW NATIONALISM

1.3.1 Political Background

The Progressive Party dissolved rapidly after the election of 1912. The Republicans made major gains in Congress and in the state governments in the 1914 elections, and their victory in 1916 seemed probable. Early in 1916 Wilson and the Democrats abandoned most of their limited government and states' rights positions in favor of a legislative program of broad economic and social reforms designed to win the support of the former Progressives for the Democratic Party in the election of 1916. The urgency of their concern was increased by the fact that Theodore Roosevelt intended to seek the Republican nomination in 1916.

1.3.2 *The Brandeis Appointment*

Wilson's first action marking the adoption of the new program was the appointment on January 28, 1916 of Louis D. Brandeis, considered by many to be the principal advocate of social justice in the nation, as an associate justice of the Supreme Court.

1.3.3 *The Federal Farm Loan Act of 1916*

The law divided the country into twelve regions and established a Federal Land Bank in each region. Funded primarily with federal money, the banks made farm mortgage loans at reasonable interest rates. Wilson had threatened to veto similar legislation in 1914.

1.3.4 *The Child Labor Act of 1916*

This law, earlier opposed by Wilson, forbade shipment in interstate commerce of products whose production had involved the labor of children under fourteen or sixteen, depending on the products. The legislation was especially significant because it was the first time that Congress regulated labor within a state using the interstate commerce power. The law was declared unconstitutional by the Supreme Court in 1918 on the grounds that it interfered with the powers of the states.

1.3.5 *The Adamson Act of 1916*

This law mandated an eight-hour day for workers on interstate railroads with time and a half for overtime and a maximum of sixteen hours in a shift. Its passage was a major victory for railroad unions, and averted a railroad strike in September 1916.

1.3.6 The Kerr-McGillicuddy Act of 1916

This law initiated a program of workmen's compensation for federal employees.

1.4 THE ELECTION OF 1916

1.4.1 The Democrats

The minority party nationally in terms of voter registration, the Democrats nominated Wilson and adopted his platform calling for continued progressive reforms and neutrality in the European war. "He kept us out of war" became the principal campaign slogan of Democratic politicians.

1.4.2 The Republicans

The convention bypassed Theodore Roosevelt, who had decided not to run as a Progressive and had sought the Republican nomination. On the first ballot it chose Charles Evans Hughes, an associate justice of the Supreme Court and formerly a progressive Republican governor of New York. Hughes, an ineffective campaigner, avoided the neutrality issue because of divisions among the Republicans, and found it difficult to attack the progressive reforms of the Democrats. He emphasized what he considered the inefficiency of the Democrats, and failed to find a popular issue.

1.4.3 The Election

Wilson won the election with 277 electoral votes and 9,129,000 popular votes, almost three million more than he received in 1912. Hughes received 254 electoral votes and 8,538,221 popular votes. The Democrats controlled Congress by a narrow margin. While Wilson's victory seemed close, the fact that he had increased his popular vote by almost fifty percent over four years previous was remarkable. It appears that most of his additional votes came from people who had voted for the Progressive or Socialist tickets in 1912.

1.5 SOCIAL ISSUES IN THE FIRST WILSON ADMINISTRATION

1.5.1 *Blacks*

In 1913 Treasury Secretary William G. McAdoo and Postmaster General Albert S. Burleson segregated workers in some parts of their departments with no objection from Wilson. Many northern blacks and whites protested, especially black leader W. E. B. DuBois, who had supported Wilson in 1912. William Monroe Trotter, militant editor of the Boston *Guardian*, led a protest delegation to Washington and clashed verbally with the president. No further segregation in government agencies was initiated, but Wilson had gained a reputation for being inimical to civil rights.

1.5.2 *Women*

The movement for woman suffrage, led by the National American Woman Suffrage Association, was increasing in momentum at the time Wilson became president, and several states had granted the vote to women. Wilson opposed a federal woman suffrage amendment, maintaining that the franchise should be controlled by the states. Later he changed his view and supported the nineteenth amendment.

1.5.4 *Immigration*

Wilson opposed immigration restrictions which were proposed by labor unions and some reformers. He vetoed a literacy test for immigrants in 1915, but in 1917 Congress overrode a similar veto.

CHAPTER 2

WILSON'S FOREIGN POLICY AND THE ROAD TO WAR

2.1 NEW FREEDOM FOREIGN POLICY

2.1.1 *Wilson's Basic Premise*

Wilson promised a more moral foreign policy than that of his predecessors, denouncing imperialism and dollar diplomacy, and advocating the advancement of democratic capitalist governments throughout the world.

2.1.2 *Conciliation Treaties*

Secretary Bryan negotiated treaties with twenty-nine nations under which they agreed to submit disputes to international commissions for conciliation, not arbitration. They also included provisions for a cooling-off period, usually one year, before the nations would resort to war. While the treaties probably had no practical effect, they illustrated the idealism of the administration.

2.1.3 Dollar Diplomacy

Wilson signaled his repudiation of Taft's dollar diplomacy by withdrawing American involvement from the six-power loan consortium of China.

2.1.4 Japan

In 1913 Wilson failed to prevent passage of a California law prohibiting land ownership by Japanese aliens. The Japanese government and people were furious, and war seemed possible. Relations were smoothed over, but the issue was unresolved. In 1915 American diplomatic pressure made Japan back off from its twenty-one demands on China, but in 1917 the Lansing-Ishii Agreement was signed wherein Japan recognized the Open Door in China but the United States recognized Japan's special interest in that nation.

2.1.5 The Caribbean

Like his predecessors, Wilson sought to protect the Panama Canal, which opened in 1914, by maintaining stability in the area. He also wanted to encourage diplomacy and economic growth in the underdeveloped nations of the region. In applying his policy, he became as interventionist as Roosevelt and Taft.

Nicaragua. In 1912 American marines had landed in Nicaragua to maintain order, and an American financial expert had taken control of the customs. The Wilson administration kept the marines in Nicaragua, and negotiated the Bryan-Chamorro Treaty of 1914 which gave the United States an option to build a canal through the country. In effect, Nicaragua became an American protectorate, although treaty provisions authorizing such action were not ratified by the Senate.

Haiti. Claiming that political anarchy existed in Haiti, Wilson sent marines in 1915 and imposed a treaty making the country a protectorate, with American control of its finances and constabulary. The marines remained until 1934.

Dominican Republic. In 1916 Wilson sent marines to the Dominican Republic to stop a civil war, and established a military government under an American naval commander.

Virgin Islands. Wilson feared in 1915 that Germany might annex Denmark and its Caribbean possession, the Danish West Indies or Virgin Islands. After extended negotiations, the United States purchased the islands from Denmark by treaty on August 4, 1916 for twenty-five million dollars, and took possession of them on March 31, 1917.

Mexico. In 1913 Wilson refused to recognize the government of Mexican military dictator Victoriano Huerta, and offered unsuccessfully to mediate between Huerta and his Constitutionalist opponent, Venustiano Carranza. When the Huerta government arrested several American seamen in Tampico in April 1914, American forces occupied the port of Veracruz, an action condemned by both Mexican political factions. In July 1914 Huerta abdicated his power to Carranza, who was soon opposed by his former general Francisco "Pancho" Villa. Seeking American intervention as a means of undermining Carranza, Villa shot sixteen Americans on a train in northern Mexico in January 1916, and burned the border town of Columbus, New Mexico, in March 1916, killing nineteen people. Carranza reluctantly consented to Wilson's request that the United States be allowed to pursue and capture Villa in Mexico, but did not expect the force of about six thousand Army troops under the command of General John J. Pershing which crossed the Rio Grande on March 18. The force advanced over three hundred miles into Mexico, failed to capture Villa, and became, in ef-

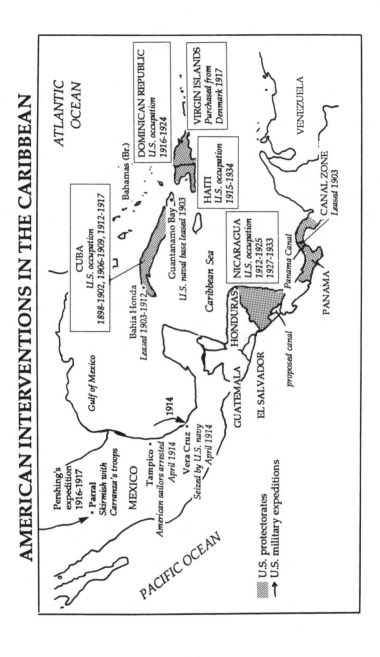

AMERICAN INTERVENTIONS IN THE CARIBBEAN

ATLANTIC OCEAN

PACIFIC OCEAN

Gulf of Mexico

MEXICO

Pershing's expedition 1916-1917

• Parral
Skirmish with Carranza's troops

Tampico •
American sailors arrested April 1914

Vera Cruz •
Seized by U.S. navy April 1914

1914

Bahamas (Br.)

CUBA
U.S. occupation
1898-1902, 1906-1909, 1912-1917

Bahia Honda
Leased 1903-1912

Guantanamo Bay
U.S. naval base leased 1903

Caribbean Sea

GUATEMALA

EL SALVADOR

HONDURAS

proposed canal

NICARAGUA
U.S. occupation
1912-1925
1927-1933

Panama Canal

PANAMA

CANAL ZONE
Leased 1903

HAITI
U.S. occupation
1915-1934

DOMINICAN REPUBLIC
U.S. occupation
1916-1924

VIRGIN ISLANDS
Purchased from
Denmark 1917

VENEZUELA

U.S. protectorates
U.S. military expeditions

14

fect, an army of occupation. The Carranza government demanded an American withdrawal, and several clashes with Mexican troops occurred. War threatened, but in January 1917 Wilson removed the American forces.

2.2 THE ROAD TO WAR IN EUROPE

2.2.1 *American Neutrality*

When World War I broke out in Europe, Wilson issued a proclamation of American neutrality on August 4, 1914. Despite that action, the United States drifted toward closer ties with the Allies, especially Britain and France. While many Americans were sympathetic to the Central Powers, the majority, including Wilson, hoped for an Allied victory. Although British naval power effectively prevented American trade with the Central Powers and European neutrals, often in violation of international law, the United States limited itself to formal diplomatic protests. The value of American trade with the Central Powers fell from $169 million in 1914 to almost nothing in 1916, but trade with the Allies rose from $825 million to $3.2 billion during the same period. In addition, the British and French had borrowed about $3.25 billion from American sources by 1917. The United States had become a major supplier of Allied munitions, food, and raw materials.

2.2.2 *The Submarine Crisis of 1915*

The Germans began the use of submarines in 1915, announced a submarine blockade of the Allies on February 4, and began to attack unarmed British passenger ships in the Atlantic. Wilson insisted to the Germans that Americans had a right as neutrals to travel safely on such ships, and that international law required a war ship to arrange for the safe removal of passengers before attacking such a ship. The sinking of the

British liner *Lusitania* off the coast of Ireland on May 7, 1915 with the loss of 1,198 lives, including 128 Americans, brought strong protests from Wilson. Secretary of State Bryan, who believed Americans should stay off belligerent ships, resigned rather than insist on questionable neutral rights, and was replaced by Robert Lansing. Following the sinking of another liner, the *Arabic*, on August 19, the Germans gave the *"Arabic* pledge" to stop attacks on unarmed passenger vessels.

2.2.3 *The Gore-McLemore Resolution*

During the latter part of 1915 the British began to arm their merchant ships. Many Americans thought it in the interest of United States neutrality that Americans not travel on the vessels of belligerents. Early in 1916 the Gore-McLemore Resolution to prohibit American travel on armed ships or on ships carrying munitions was introduced in Congress, but it was defeated in both houses after intensive politicking by Wilson.

2.2.4 *The* Sussex *Pledge*

When the unarmed French channel steamer *Sussex* was torpedoed but not sunk on March 24, 1916 with seven Americans injured, Wilson threatened to sever relations unless Germany ceased all surprise submarine attacks on all shipping, whether belligerent or neutral, armed or unarmed. Germany acceded with the *"Sussex* pledge" at the beginning of May, but threatened to resume submarine warfare if the British did not stop their violations of international law.

2.2.5 *The House-Grey Memorandum*

Early in 1915 Wilson sent his friend and adviser, Colonel Edward M. House, on an unsuccessful visit to the capitals of the belligerent nations on both sides to offer American mediation in the war. Late in the year House returned to London to propose that Wilson call a peace conference, and, if Germany refused to attend or was uncooperative at the conference, the United States would probably enter the war on the Allied side. An agreement to that effect, called the House-Grey Memorandum, was signed by the British foreign secretary, Sir Edward Gray, on February 22, 1916.

2.2.6 Preparedness

In November 1915 Wilson proposed a major increase in the Army and the abolition of the National Guard as a preparedness measure. Americans divided on the issue, with organizations like the National Security League proposing stronger military forces, and others like the League to Enforce Peace opposing. After opposition by southern and western antipreparedness Democrats, Congress passed a modified National Defense Act in June 1916 which increased the Army from about 90,000 to 220,000, and enlarged the National Guard under federal control. In August over $500 million were appropriated for naval construction. The additional costs were met by increased taxes on the wealthy.

2.2.7 The Election of 1916

This election is covered in more detail in Chapter 1.4. Wilson took the leadership on the peace issue, charging that the Republicans were the war party and that the election of Charles Evans Hughes would probably result in war with Germany and Mexico. His position was popular with many Democrats and progressives, and the slogan "He kept us out of war" became the principal theme of Democratic campaign materials, presumably contributing to his election victory.

2.2.8 Wilson's Final Peace Efforts, 1916 – 1917

On December 12, 1916 the Germans, confident of their strong position, proposed a peace conference, a step which Wilson previously had advocated. When Wilson asked both sides to state their expectations, the British seemed agreeable to reasonable negotiations, but the Germans were evasive and stated that they did not want Wilson at the conference. In an address to Congress on January 22, 1917, Wilson made his last offer to serve as a neutral mediator. He proposed a "peace without victory," based not on a "balance of power" but on a "community of power," alluding to his proposal of May 1916 for an "association of nations."

2.2.9 Unlimited Submarine Warfare

Germany announced on January 31, 1917 that it would sink all ships, belligerent or neutral, without warning in a large war zone off the coasts of the Allied nations in the eastern Atlantic and the Mediterranean. The Germans realized that the United States might declare war, but they believed that, after cutting the flow of supplies to the Allies, they could win the war before the Americans could send any sizable force to Europe. Wilson broke diplomatic relations with Germany on February 3. During February and March several American merchant ships were sunk by submarines.

2.2.10 The Zimmerman Telegram

The British intercepted a secret message from the German foreign secretary, Arthur Zimmerman, to the German minister in Mexico, and turned it over to the United States on February 24, 1917. The Germans proposed that, in the event of a war between the United States and Germany, Mexico attack the United States. After the war, the "lost territories" of Texas, New Mexico, and Arizona would be returned to Mexico. In addition,

Japan would be invited to join the alliance against the United States. When the telegram was released to the press on March 1, many Americans became convinced that war with Germany was necessary.

2.2.11 *The Declaration of War*

Wilson, on March 2, 1917, called Congress to a special session beginning April 2. When Congress convened, he requested a declaration of war against Germany. The declaration was passed by the Senate on April 4 by a vote of 82 to 6, by the House on April 6 by a vote of 373 to 50, and signed by Wilson on April 6.

2.2.12 *Wilson's Reasons*

Wilson's decision to ask for a declaration of war seems to have been based primarily on four considerations:

1) He believed that the Zimmerman Telegram showed that the Germans were not trustworthy and would eventually go to war against the United States.

2) He felt that armed neutrality could not adequately protect American shipping.

3) The democratic government established in Russia after the revolution in March 1917 was more acceptable as an ally than the Tsarist government.

4) He was convinced that the United States could hasten the end of the war and insure for itself a major role in designing a lasting peace.

CHAPTER 3

WORLD WAR I

3.1 THE MILITARY CAMPAIGN

3.1.1 *Raising an Army*

Despite the enlistment of many volunteers, it was apparent that a draft would be necessary. The Selective Service Act was passed on May 18, 1917 after bitter opposition in the House led by the speaker, "Champ" Clark. Only a compromise outlawing the sale of liquor in or near military camps secured passage. Originally including all males twenty-one to thirty, the limits were later extended to seventeen and forty-six. The first drawing of 500,000 names was made on July 20, 1917. By the end of the war 24,231,021 men had been registered and 2,810,296 had been inducted. In addition, about two million men and women volunteered.

3.1.2 *Women and Minorities in the Military*

Some women served as clerks in the navy or in the Signal Corps of the army. Originally nurses were part of the Red Cross, but eventually some were taken into the army. About

400,000 black men were drafted or enlisted, despite the objections of southern political leaders. They were kept in segregated units, usually with white officers, which were used as labor battalions or for other support activities. Some black units did see combat, and a few blacks became officers, but did not command white troops.

3.1.3 *The War at Sea*

In 1917 German submarines sank 6.5 million tons of Allied and American shipping, while only 2.7 million tons were built. German hopes for victory were based on the destruction of Allied supply lines. The American navy furnished destroyers to fight the submarines, and, after overcoming great resistance from the British navy, finally began the use of the convoy system in July 1917. Shipping losses fell from almost 900,000 tons in April 1917 to about 400,000 tons in December 1917, and remained below 200,000 tons per month after April 1918. The American navy transported over 900,000 American soldiers to France, while British transports carried over one million. Only two of the well-guarded troop transports were sunk. The navy had over two thousand ships and over half a million men by the end of the war.

3.1.4 *The American Expeditionary Force*

The soldiers and marines sent to France under command of Major General John J. Pershing were called the American Expeditionary Force, or the AEF. From a small initial force which arrived in France in June 1917, the AEF increased to over two million by November 1918. Pershing resisted efforts by European commanders to amalgamate the Americans with the French and British armies, insisting that he maintain a separate command. American casualties included 112,432 dead, about half of whom died of disease, and 230,024 wounded.

3.1.5 *Major Military Engagements*

The American force of about 14,500 which had arrived in France by September 1917 was assigned a quiet section of the line near Verdun. As numbers increased, the American role became more significant. When the Germans mounted a major drive toward Paris in the spring of 1918, the Americans experienced their first important engagements. In June they prevented the Germans from crossing the Marne at Chateau-Thierry, and cleared the area of Belleau Woods. In July, eight American divisions aided French troops in attacking the German line between Reims and Soissons. The American First Army with over half a million men under Pershing's immediate command was assembled in August 1918, and began a major offensive at St. Mihiel on the southern part of the front on September 12. Following the successful operation, Pershing began a drive against the German defenses between Verdun and Sedan, an action called the Meuse-Argonne offensive, and reached Sedan on November 7. During the same period the English in the north and the French along the central front also broke through the German lines. The fighting ended with the armistice on November 11, 1918.

3.2   MOBILIZING THE HOME FRONT

3.2.1 *Industry*

The Council of National Defense, comprised of six cabinet members and a seven-member advisory commission of business and labor leaders, was established in 1916 before American entry into the war to coordinate industrial mobilization, but it had little authority. In July 1917 the council created the War Industries Board to control raw materials, production, prices, and labor relations. The military forces refused to cooperate with the civilian agency in purchasing their supplies, and the

THE AMERICAN EXPEDITIONARY FORCE, 1918

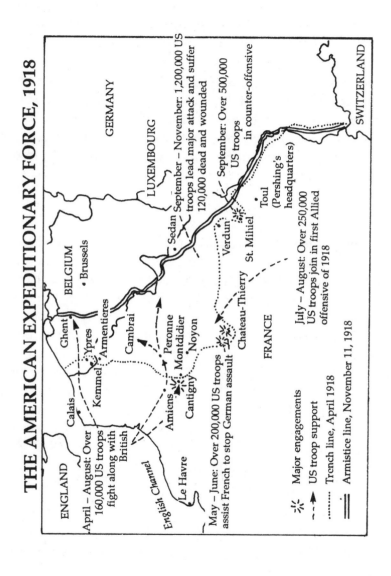

April – August: Over 160,000 US troops fight along with British

May – June: Over 200,000 US troops assist French to stop German assault

July – August: Over 250,000 US troops join in first Allied offensive of 1918

September – November: 1,200,000 US troops lead major attack and suffer 120,000 dead and wounded

September: Over 500,000 US troops in counter-offensive

ENGLAND

BELGIUM

GERMANY

LUXEMBOURG

FRANCE

SWITZERLAND

English Channel

Le Havre

Calais

Ghent

Ypres
Kemmel
Armentieres

Cambrai

Amiens

Cantigny

Peronne
Montdidier
Noyon

Chateau-Thierry

St. Mihiel

Verdun

Sedan

Toul
(Pershing's headquarters)

Brussels

⚡ Major engagements

- - → US troop support

········· Trench line, April 1918

‖‖ Armistice line, November 11, 1918

domestic war effort seemed on the point of collapse in December 1917 when a Congressional investigation began. In 1918 Wilson took stronger action under his emergency war powers which were reinforced by the Overman Act of May 1918. In March 1918 Wilson appointed Wall Street broker Bernard M. Baruch to head the WIB, assisted by an advisory committee of one hundred businessmen. The WIB allocated raw materials, standardized manufactured products, instituted strict production and purchasing controls, and paid high prices to businesses for their products. Even so, American industry was just beginning to produce heavy armaments when the war ended. Most heavy equipment and munitions used by the American troops in France were produced in Britain or France.

3.2.2 Food

The United States had to supply not only its own food needs but those of Britain, France, and some of the other Allies as well. The problem was compounded by bad weather in 1916 and 1917 which had an adverse effect on agriculture. The Lever Act of 1917 gave the president broad control over the production, price, and distribution of food and fuel. Herbert Hoover was appointed by Wilson to head a newly-created Food Administration. Hoover fixed high prices to encourage the production of wheat, pork, and other products, and encouraged the conservation of food through such voluntary programs as "Wheatless Mondays" and "Meatless Tuesdays." Despite the bad harvests in 1916 and 1917, food exports by 1919 were almost triple those of the prewar years, and real farm income was up almost thirty percent.

3.2.3 Fuel

The Fuel Administration under Harry A. Garfield was established in August 1917. It was concerned primarily with coal production and conservation because coal was the predominant fuel of the time and was in short supply during the severe winter of 1917 – 1918. "Fuelless Mondays" in nonessential industries to conserve coal and "Gasless Sundays" for automobile owners to save gasoline were instituted. Coal production increased about thirty-five percent from 1914 to 1918.

3.2.4 Railroads

The American railroad system, which provided most of the inter-city transportation in the country, seemed near collapse in December 1917 because the wartime demands and heavy snows which slowed service. Wilson created the United States Railroad Administration under William G. McAdoo, the secretary of the Treasury, to take over and operate all the railroads in the nation as one system. The government paid the owners rent for the use of their lines, spent over $500 million on improved tracks and equipment, and achieved its objective of an efficient railroad system.

3.2.5 Maritime Shipping

The United States Shipping Board was authorized by Congress in September 1916, and in April 1917 it created a subsidiary, the Emergency Fleet Corporation, to buy, build, lease, and operate merchant ships for the war effort. Edward N. Hurley became the director in July 1917, and the corporation constructed several large shipyards which were just beginning to produce vessels when the war ended. By seizing German and Dutch ships, and by the purchase and requisition of private vessels, the board had accumulated a large fleet by September 1918.

3.2.6 Labor

To prevent strikes and work stoppages in war industries, the War Labor Board was created in April 1918 under the joint chairmanship of former president William Howard Taft and attorney Frank P. Walsh with members from both industry and labor. In hearing labor disputes the WLB in effect prohibited strikes, but it also encouraged higher wages, the eight-hour day, and unionization. Union membership doubled during the war from about 2.5 million to about 5 million.

3.2.7   War Finance and Taxation

The war is estimated to have cost about $33.5 billion by 1920, excluding such future costs as veterans' benefits and debt service. Of that amount at least $7 billion was loaned to the Allies, with most of the money actually spent in the United States for supplies. The government raised about $10.5 billion in taxes, and borrowed the remaining $23 billion. Taxes were raised substantially in 1917, and again in 1918. The Revenue Act of 1918, which did not take effect until 1919, imposed a personal income tax of six percent on incomes to $4,000, and twelve percent on incomes above that amount. In addition, a graduated surtax went to a maximum of 65 percent on large incomes, for a total of 77 percent. Corporations paid an excess profits tax of 65 percent, and excise taxes were levied on luxury items. Much public, peer, and employer pressure was exerted on citizens to buy Liberty Bonds which covered a major part of the borrowing. An inflation of about one hundred percent from 1915 to 1920 contributed substantially to the cost of the war.

3.3   PUBLIC OPINION AND CIVIL LIBERTIES

3.3.1   The Committee on Public Information

The committee, headed by journalist George Creel, was formed by Wilson in April 1917. Creel established a successful system of voluntary censorship of the press, and organized about 150,000 paid and volunteer writers, lecturers, artists, and other professionals in a propaganda campaign to build support for the American cause as an idealistic crusade, and to portray the Germans as barbaric and beastial Huns. The CPI set up volunteer Liberty Leagues in every community, and urged their members, and citizens at large, to spy on their neighbors, especially those with foreign names, and to report any suspicious words or actions to the Justice Department.

3.3.2 War Hysteria

A number of volunteer organizations sprang up around the country to search for draft dodgers, enforce the sale of bonds, and report any opinion or conversation considered suspicious. Perhaps the largest such organization was the American Protective League with about 250,000 members, which claimed the approval of the Justice Department. Such groups publicly humiliated people accused of not buying war bonds and persecuted, beat, and sometimes killed people of German descent. As a result of the activities of the CPI and the vigilante groups, German language instruction and German music were banned in many areas, German measles became "liberty measles," pretzels were prohibited in some cities, and the like. The anti-German and anti-subversive war hysteria in the United States far exceeded similar public moods in Britain and France during the war.

3.3.3 The Espionage and Sedition Acts

The Espionage Act of 1917 provided for fines and imprisonment for persons who made false statements which aided the enemy, incited rebellion in the military, or obstructed recruitment or the draft. Printed matter advocating treason or insurrection could be excluded from the mails. The Sedition Act of May 1918 forbade any criticism of the government, flag, or uniform, even if there were not detrimental consequences, and expanded the mail exclusion. The laws sounded reasonable, but they were applied in ways which trampled on civil liberties.

Eugene V. Debs, the perennial Socialist candidate for president, was given a ten-year prison sentence for a speech at his party's convention in which he was critical of American policy in entering the war and warned of the dangers of militarism. Movie producer Robert Goldstein released the movie *The Spirit of '76* about the Revolutionary War. It naturally showed the British fighting the Americans. Goldstein was fined $10,000 and sentenced to ten years in prison because the film depicted the British, who were now fighting on the same side as the United States, in an unfavorable light. The Espionage Act was upheld by the Supreme Court in the case of *Shenk v. United States* in 1919. The opinion, written by Justice Oliver Wendell Holmes, Jr., stated that Congress could limit free speech when the words represented a "clear and present danger," and that a person cannot cry "fire" in a crowded theater. The Sedition Act was similarly upheld in *Abrams v. United States* a few months later. Ultimately 2,168 persons were prosecuted under the laws, and 1,055 were convicted, of whom only ten were charged with actual sabotage.

3.4   WARTIME SOCIAL TRENDS

3.4.1 *Women*

With approximately sixteen percent of the normal labor force in uniform and demand for goods at a peak, large numbers of women, mostly white, were hired by factories and other enterprises in jobs never before open to them. They were often resented and ridiculed by male workers. When the war ended, almost all returned to traditional "women's jobs" or to homemaking. Returning veterans replaced them in the labor market. Women continued to campaign for woman suffrage. In 1917 six states, including the large and influential states of New York, Ohio, Indiana, and Michigan, gave the vote to women. Wilson changed his position in 1918 to advocate woman suffrage as a war measure. In January 1918 the House of Representatives adopted a suffrage amendment to the constitution which was defeated later in the year by southern forces in the Senate. The way was paved for the victory of the suffragists after the war.

3.4.2 Racial Minorities

The labor shortage opened industrial jobs to Mexican-Americans and to blacks. W. E. B. DuBois, the most prominent black leader of the time, supported the war effort in the hope that the war to make the world safe for democracy would bring a better life for blacks in the United States. About half a million rural southern blacks migrated to cities, mainly in the North and Midwest, to obtain employment in war and other industries, especially in steel and meatpacking. Some white southerners, fearing the loss of labor when cotton prices were high, tried forceably to prevent their departure. Some white northerners, fearing job competition and encroachment on white neighborhoods, resented their arrival. In 1917 there were race riots in twenty-six cities North and South, with the worst in East St. Louis, Illinois. Despite the opposition and their concentration in entry-level positions, there is evidence that the blacks who migrated generally improved themselves economically.

3.4.3 Prohibition

Proponents of prohibition stressed the need for military personnel to be sober and the need to conserve grain for food, and depicted the hated Germans as disgusting beer drinkers. In December 1917 a constitutional amendment to prohibit the manufacture and sale of alcoholic beverages in the United States was passed by Congress and submitted to the states for ratification. While alcohol consumption was being attacked, cigarette consumption climbed from twenty-six billion in 1916 to forty-eight billion in 1918.

CHAPTER 4

PEACEMAKING AND DOMESTIC PROBLEMS, 1918 – 1920

4.1   PEACEMAKING

4.1.1   *The Fourteen Points*

From the time of the American entry into the war, Wilson had maintained that the war would make the world safe for democracy. He insisted that there should be peace without victory, meaning that the victors would not be vindictive toward the losers, so that a fair and stable international situation in the postwar world would insure lasting peace. In an address to Congress on January 8, 1918 he presented his specific peace plan in the form of the Fourteen Points. The first five points called for open rather than secret peace treaties, freedom of the seas, free trade, arms reduction, and a fair adjustment of colonial claims. The next eight points were concerned with the national aspirations of various European peoples and the adjustment of boundaries, as, for example, in the creation of an independent Poland. The fourteenth point, which he considered the most important and had espoused as early as 1916, called for a "general association of nations" to preserve the peace. The plan was disdained by the Allied leadership, but it had great appeal for many people on both sides of the conflict in Europe and America.

4.1.2 The Election of 1918

On October 25, 1918, a few days before the congressional elections, Wilson appealed to the voters to elect a Democratic Congress, saying that to do otherwise would be a repudiation of his leadership in European affairs. Republicans, who had loyally supported his war programs, were affronted. The voters, probably influenced more by domestic and local issues than by foreign policy, gave the Republicans a slim margin in both houses in the election. Wilson's statement had undermined his political support at home and his stature in the eyes of world leaders.

4.1.3 The Armistice

The German Chancellor, Prince Max of Baden, on October 3, 1918 asked Wilson to begin peace negotiations based on his concepts of a just peace and the Fourteen Points. Wilson insisted that the Germans must evacuate Belgium and France and form a civilian government. By early November the Allied and American armies were advancing rapidly and Germany was on the verge of collapse. The German Emperor fled to the Netherlands and abdicated. Representatives of the new German republic signed the armistice on November 11, 1918 to be effective at 11:00 A.M. that day, and agreed to withdraw German forces to the Rhine and to surrender military equipment, including 150 submarines.

4.1.4 *The Versailles or Paris Peace Conference*

Wilson decided that he would lead the American delegation to the peace conference which opened in Paris on January 12, 1919. The other members of the delegation were Secretary of State Robert Lansing, General Tasker Bliss, Colonel Edward M. House, and attorney Henry White. Wilson made a serious mistake in not appointing any leading Republicans to the commission and in not consulting the Republican leadership in the Senate about the negotiations. In Paris, Wilson joined Prime Minister David Lloyd George of Great Britain, Premier Georges Clemenceau of France, and Prime Minister Vittorio Orlando of Italy to form the "Big Four" which dominated the conference. In the negotiations, which continued until May 1919, Wilson found it necessary to make many compromises in forging the text of the treaty.

4.1.5 *The Soviet Influence*

Russia was the only major participant in the war which was not represented at the peace conference. Following the Communist Revolution of 1917, Russia had made a separate peace with Germany in March 1918. Wilson had resisted Allied plans to send major military forces to Russia to oust the Communists and bring Russia back into the war. An American force of about five thousand was sent to Murmansk in the summer of 1918 in association with British and French troops to prevent the Germans from taking military supplies, and was soon active in assisting Russian anti-Bolsheviks. It remained in the area until June 1919. In July 1918 Wilson also sent about ten thousand soldiers to Siberia where they took over the operation of the railroads to assist a Czech army which was escaping from the Germans by crossing Russia. They were also to counterbalance a larger Japanese force in the area, and remained until April 1920. Wilson believed that the spread of communism was the greatest threat to peace and international order. His concern made him reluctant to dispute too much with the other leaders at the Versailles Conference, and more agreeable to compromise, because he believed it imperative that the democracies remain united in the face of the communist threat.

4.1.6 *Important Provisions of the Versailles Treaty*

In the drafting of the treaty Wilson achieved some of the goals in the Fourteen Points, compromised on others, and failed to secure freedom of the seas, free trade, reduction of armaments, or the return of Russia to the society of free nations. Some major decisions were as follows:

1) The League of Nations was formed, implementing the point which Wilson considered the most important. Article X of the Covenant, or charter, of the League called on all members to protect the "territorial integrity" and "political independence" of all other members.

2) Germany was held responsible for causing the war; required to agree to pay the Allies for all civilian damage and veterans' costs, which eventually were calculated at $33 billion; the German army and navy were limited to tiny defensive forces; and the west bank of the Rhine was declared a military-free zone forever and occupied by the French for fifteen years. These decisions were clearly contrary to the idea of peace without victory.

3) New nations of Yugoslavia, Austria, Hungary, Czechoslovakia, Poland, Lithuania, Latvia, Estonia, and Finland partially fulfilled the idea of self-determination for all nationalities, but the boundaries drawn at the conference left many people under the control of other nationalities.

4) German colonies were made mandates of the League of

Nations, and given in trusteeship to France, Japan, and Britain and its Dominions.

4.1.7 *Germany and the Signing of the Treaty*

The German delegates were allowed to come to Versailles in May 1919 after the completion of the treaty document. They expected to negotiate on the basis of the draft, but were told to sign it "or else," probably meaning an economic boycott of Germany. They protested, but signed the Versailles Treaty on June 28, 1919.

4.1.8 *The Senate and the Treaty*

Following a protest by thirty-nine senators in February 1919, Wilson obtained some changes in the League structure to exempt the Monroe Doctrine and domestic matters from League jurisdiction. Then, on July 26, 1919, he presented the treaty with the League within it to the Senate for ratification. Almost all of the forty-seven Democrats supported Wilson and the treaty, but the forty-nine Republicans were divided. About a dozen were "irreconcilables" who thought that the United States should not be a member of the League under any circumstances. The remainder included twenty-five "strong" and twelve "mild" reservationists who would accept the treaty with some changes. The main objection centered on Article X of the League Covenant, where the reservationists wanted it understood that the United States would not go to war to defend a League member without the approval of Congress. The leader of the reservationists was Henry Cabot Lodge of Massachusetts, the chairman of the Foreign Relations Committee. More senators than the two-thirds necessary for ratification favored the treaty either as written or with reservations.

4.1.9 *Wilson and the Senate*

On September 3, 1919 Wilson set out on a national speaking tour to appeal to the people to support the treaty and the League, and to influence their senators. He collapsed after a speech in Pueblo, Colorado, on September 25, and returned to Washington where he suffered a severe stroke on October 2 which paralyzed his left side. He was seriously ill for several months, and never fully recovered. In a letter to the Senate Democrats on November 18, Wilson urged them to oppose the treaty with the Lodge reservations. In votes the next day, the treaty failed to get a two-thirds majority either with or without the reservations.

4.1.10 *The Final Vote*

Many people, including British and French leaders, urged Wilson to compromise with Lodge on reservations, including the issue of Article X. Wilson, instead, wrote an open letter to Democrats on January 8, 1920 urging them to make the election of a Democratic president in 1920 a "great and solemn referendum" on the treaty as written. Such partisanship only acerbated the situation. Many historians think that Wilson's ill health impaired his judgment, and that he would have worked out a compromise had he not had the stroke. The Senate took up the treaty again in February 1920, and on March 19 it was again defeated both with and without the reservations. The United States officially ended the war with Germany by a resolution of Congress signed on July 2, 1921, and a separate peace treaty was ratified on July 25. The United States did not join the League.

4.2 DOMESTIC PROBLEMS AND THE END OF THE WILSON ADMINISTRATION

4.2.1 Demobilization

The AEF was brought home as quickly as possible in early 1919, and members of the armed forces were rapidly discharged. Congress provided for wounded veterans through a system of veteran's hospitals under the Veteran's Bureau, and funded relief, especially food supplies, for war-torn Europe. The wartime agencies for the control of the economy, such as the War Industries Board, were soon disbanded. During 1919 Congress considered various plans to nationalize the railroads or continue their public operation, but then passed the Esch-Cummings or Transportation Act of 1920 which returned them to private ownership and operation. It did extend Interstate Commerce Commission control over their rates and financial affairs, and allowed supervised pooling. The fleet of ships accumulated by the Shipping Board during the war was sold to private owners at attractive prices.

4.2.2 Final Reforms of the Progressive Era

In January 1919 the Eighteenth Amendment to the Constitution prohibiting the manufacture, sale, transportation, or importation of intoxicating liquors was ratified by the states, and it became effective in January 1920. The Nineteenth Amendment providing for woman suffrage, which had been defeated in the Senate in 1918, was approved by Congress in 1919. It was ratified by the states in time for the election of 1920.

4.2.3 The Postwar Economy

Despite fear of unemployment with the return of veterans to the labor force and the end of war purchases, the American economy boomed during 1919 and the first half of 1920. Consumers had money from high wages during the war, and the European demand for American food and manufactured products continued for some months after the war. The demand for goods resulted in a rapid inflation. Prices in 1919 were 77 percent above the prewar level, and in 1920 there were 105 percent above that level.

4.2.4 Strikes

The great increase in prices prompted 2,655 strikes in 1919 involving about four million workers or twenty percent of the labor force. Unions were encouraged by the gains they had made during the war and thought they had the support of public opinion. However, the Communist Revolution in Russia in 1917 soon inspired in many Americans, including government officials, a fear of violence and revolution by workers. While most of the strikes in early 1919 were successful, the tide of opinion gradually shifted against the workers. Four major strikes received particular attention:

1) *The Seattle General Strike.* In January 1919 all unions in Seattle declared a general strike in support of a strike for higher pay by shipyard workers. The action was widely condemned, the federal government sent marines, and the strike was soon abandoned.

2) *The Boston Police Strike.* In September 1919 Boston police struck for the right to unionize. Governor Calvin Coolidge called out the National Guard and stated that there was "no right to strike against the public safety by anybody, anywhere, anytime." The police were fired and a new force was recruited.

3) *The Steel Strike.* The American Federation of Labor attempted to organize the steel industry in 1919. When

Judge Elbert H. Gary, the head of U.S. Steel, refused to negotiate, the workers struck in September. After much violence and the use of federal and state troops, the strike was broken by January 1920.

4) *The Coal Strike.* The United Mine Workers of America under John L. Lewis struck for shorter hours and higher wages on November 1, 1919. Attorney General A. Mitchell Palmer obtained injunctions and the union called off the strike. An arbitration board later awarded the miners a wage increase.

4.2.5 *The Red Scare*

Americans feared the spread of the Russian Communist Revolution to the United States, and many interpreted the widespread strikes of 1919 as communist-inspired and the beginning of the revolution. Bombs sent through the mail to prominent government and business leaders in April 1919 seemed to confirm their fears, although the origin of the bombs has never been determined. The membership of the two communist parties founded in the United States in 1919 was less than one hundred thousand, but many Americans were sure that many workers, all foreign-born persons, radicals, and members of the International Workers of the World, a radical union in the western states, were communists. The anti-German hysteria of the war years was transformed into the anti-communist and anti-foreign hysteria of 1919 and 1920, and continued in various forms through the twenties.

4.2.6 *The Palmer Raids*

Attorney General A. Mitchell Palmer was one of the targets of the anonymous bombers in the spring of 1919. He was also an aspirant for the Democratic nomination for president in 1920, and he realized that many Americans saw the threat of a communist revolution as a grave danger. In August 1919 he named J. Edgar Hoover to head a new Intelligence Division in the Justice Department to collect information about radicals. In November 1919 Palmer's agents arrested almost seven hundred persons, mostly anarchists, and deported forty-three of them as undesirable aliens. On January 2, 1920 Justice Department agents, local police, and vigilantes in thirty-three cities arrested about four thousand people accused of being communists. It appears that many people caught in the sweep were neither communists nor aliens. Eventually 556 were shown to be communists and aliens, and were deported. Palmer then announced that huge communist riots were planned for major cities on May Day, May 1, 1920. Police and troops were alerted, but the day passed with no radical activity. Palmer was discredited and the Red Scare subsided.

4.2.7 *The Race Riots of 1919*

During the war about half a million blacks had migrated from the South to industrial cities, mostly in the North and Midwest, to find employment. After the war white hostility based on competition for lower-paid jobs and black encroachment into neighborhoods led to race riots in twenty-five cities with hundreds killed or wounded and millions of dollars in property damage. Beginning in Longview, Texas, the riots spread, among other places, to Washington, D.C., and Chicago. The Chicago riot in July was the worst, lasting 13 days and leaving 38 dead, 520 wounded, and 1,000 families homeless. Fear of returning black veterans in the South lead to an increase of lynchings from 34 in 1917 to 60 in 1918 and 70 in 1919. Some of the victims were veterans still in uniform.

4.3   THE ELECTION OF 1920

4.3.1   *The Political Climate*

It seemed to many political observers in 1920 that the Republicans had an excellent chance of victory. The Wilson administration was blamed by many for the wartime civil liberties abuses, the League of Nations controversy, and the strikes and inflation of the postwar period.

4.3.2   *The Republican Convention*

The principal contenders for the nomination were General Leonard Wood, who had the support of the followers of the deceased Theodore Roosevelt, and Governor Frank O. Lowden of Illinois, the pick of many of the party bosses. When the convention seemed to deadlock, Henry Cabot Lodge, the convention chairman, and several other leaders arranged for the name of Senator Warren G. Harding of Ohio to be introduced as a dark-horse candidate. Harding was nominated on the tenth ballot, and Governor Calvin Coolidge of Massachusetts was chosen as the vice presidential nominee. The platform opposed the League, and promised low taxes, high tariffs, immigration restriction, and aid to farmers.

4.3.3   *The Democratic Convention*

The front-runners were William Gibbs McAdoo, the secretary of the Treasury and Wilson's son-in-law, and Attorney General A. Mitchell Palmer. Governor James Cox of Ohio was entered as a favorite son. Wilson expected the convention to deadlock, at which point his name would be introduced and he would be nominated for a third term by acclamation. His plan never materialized. McAdoo and Palmer contended for thirty-seven ballots with neither receiving the two-thirds necessary for nomination. Palmer then released his delegates, most of whom turned to Cox. Cox was nominated on the forty-fourth ballot, and Franklin D. Roosevelt, an assistant secretary of the Navy and distant cousin of Theodore, was selected as his running mate. The platform endorsed the League, but left the door open for reservations.

4.3.4 *The Campaign*

Harding's managers decided that he should speak as little as possible, but he did address visiting delegations from his front porch in Marion, Ohio. It was impossible to tell where he stood on the League issue, but he struck a responsive chord in many people when he urged that the nation should abandon heroics, nostrums, and experiment, and return to what he called normalcy. Cox and Roosevelt travelled extensively, speaking mostly in support of the League. Many found neither presidential candidate impressive.

4.3.5 *The Election*

Harding received 16,152,200 popular votes, 61 percent of the total, for 404 electoral votes. Cox received 9,147,353 popular votes for 127 electoral votes. Socialist candidate Eugene V. Debs, in federal prison in Atlanta for an Espionage Act conviction, received 919,799 votes. The Democrats carried only states in the Solid South, and even there lost Tennessee. It appears that people voted Republican more as a repudiation of Wilson's domestic policies than as a referendum on the League. Wilson had alienated German-Americans, Irish-Americans, antiwar progressives, civil libertarians, and midwestern farmers, all groups which had given the Democrats considerable support in 1916.

CHAPTER 5

THE TWENTIES: ECONOMIC ADVANCES AND SOCIAL TENSIONS

5.1   THE ECONOMY OF THE TWENTIES

5.1.1   *The Recession of 1920 – 1921*

The United States experienced a severe recession from mid-1920 until the end of 1921. Europe returned to normal and reduced its purchases in America, and domestic demand for goods not available in wartime was filled. Prices fell, and unemployment exceeded twelve percent in 1921.

5.1.2   *Prosperity and Industrial Productivity*

The economy improved rapidly in 1922, and continued to be strong until 1929. Improved industrial efficiency which resulted in lower prices for goods was primarily responsible. Manufacturing output increased about sixty-five percent, and productivity, or output per hour of work, increased about forty percent. The number of industrial workers actually decreased from 9 million to 8.8 million during the decade. The increased productivity resulted from improved machinery, which in turn came about for several reasons. Industry changed from steam to electric power, allowing the design of more intricate machines which replaced the work of human hands. By 1929, seventy percent of industrial power came from electricity. The moving assembly line, first introduced by Henry Ford in the automobile industry in 1913 and 1914, was widely adopted. Scientific management, exemplified by the time and motion studies pioneered by Frederick W. Taylor before the war, led to more efficient use of workers and lower labor costs. Larger firms began, for the first time, to fund major research and development activities to find new and improved products, reduce production costs, utilize by-products, and the like.

5.1.3 *The Automobile*

The principal driving force of the economy of the twenties was the automobile. There were 8,131,522 motor vehicles registered in the United States in 1920, and 26,704,825 in 1929. Annual output of automobiles reached 3.6 million in 1923, and remained at about that level throughout the decade. By 1925 the price of a Ford Model T had been reduced to $290, less than three months pay for an average worker. Ford plants produced nine thousand Model Ts per day, and Henry Ford cleared about $25,000 a day throughout the decade. Automobile manufacturing stimulated supporting industries such as steel, rubber, and glass, as well as gasoline refining and highway construction. It was during the twenties that the United States became a nation of paved roads. Mileage of paved roads increased from 387,000 miles in 1921, most of which was in urban areas, to 662,000 in 1929. Highway construction costs averaged over one billion dollars a year in the late twenties, in part due to the Federal Highway Act of 1916 which started the federal highway system and gave matching funds to the states for construction. One estimate stated that the automobile industry directly or indirectly employed 3.7 million people in 1929.

5.1.4 *Other Leading Industries*

The electrical industry also expanded rapidly during the twenties. The demand for power for industrial machinery as well as for business and some lighting increased dramatically, and a host of electrical appliances such as stoves, vacuum cleaners, refrigerators, toasters, and radios became available. About two-thirds of American homes had electricity by 1929, leaving only those in rural areas without it. Home and business construction also experienced a boom from 1922 until 1928. Other large industries which grew rapidly were chemicals and printing. The movie industry expanded rapidly, especially after the introduction of sound films, and employed about 325,000 people by 1930. New industries which began in the period were radio and commercial aviation.

5.1.5 *Consumer Credit and Advertising*

Unlike earlier boom periods which had involved large expenditures for capital investments such as railroads and factories, the prosperity of the twenties depended heavily on the sale of consumer products. Purchases of "big ticket" items such as automobiles, refrigerators, and furniture were made possible by installment or time payment credit. The idea was not new, but the availability of consumer credit expanded tremendously during the twenties. Consumer interest and demand was spurred by the great increase in professional advertising using newspapers, magazines, radio, billboards, and other media. By 1929 advertising expenditures reached $3.4 billion, more than was spent on education at all levels.

5.1.6　The Dominance of Big Business

There was a trend toward corporate consolidation during the twenties. By 1929 the two hundred largest corporations held 49 percent of the corporate wealth and received 43 percent of corporate income. The top 5 percent of the corporations in the nation received about 85 percent of the corporate income. Corporate profits and dividends increased about 65 percent during the decade. In most fields an oligopoly of two to four firms dominated, exemplified by the automobile industry where Ford, General Motors, and Chrysler produced 83 percent of the vehicles in 1929. Firms in many fields formed trade associations which represented their interests to the public and the government, and which claimed to stabilize each industry. Government regulatory agencies such as the Federal Trade Commission and the Interstate Commerce Commission were passive and generally controlled by persons from the business world. The public generally accepted the situation and viewed the businessmen with respect. Illustrating the attitudes of the time, *The Man Nobody Knows*, a book by advertising executive Bruce Barton published in 1925, became a best-seller. It described Jesus as the founder of modern business and his apostles as an exemplary business management team.

5.1.7　Banking and Finance

As with other corporations, there was a trend toward bank consolidation. Bank assets increased about 66 percent from 1919 to 1929. There was a growth in branch banking, and in 1929 the 3.2 percent of the banks with branch operations controlled 46 percent of the banking resources. Because corporations were raising much of their money through the sale of stocks and bonds, the demand for business loans declined. Commercial banks then put more of their funds into real estate loans, loans to brokers against stocks and bonds, and the purchase of stocks and bonds themselves. By doing so they made themselves vulnerable to economic disaster when the depression began in late 1929. Even during the prosperous twenties, 5,714 banks failed, most of them in rural areas or in Florida. Banks in operation in 1929 numbered 25,568.

5.1.8 *Labor*

The National Association of Manufacturers and its state affiliates began a drive in 1920 to restore the "open shop" or nonunion workplace. The alternative used was "welfare capitalism" whereby the firm sought to provide job satisfaction so that the workers would not want a union. Company-sponsored pension and insurance plans, stock purchase plans, efforts to insure worker safety and comfort, social and sporting events, and company magazines were undertaken. Company unions, designed to give workers some voice with management under company control, were organized by 317 firms. The American Federation of Labor and other unions, which had prospered during World War I, found themselves on the defensive. Leaders, especially William Green, president of the American Federation of Labor after 1924, were conservative and nonaggressive. Union membership dropped about twenty percent from five million to about four million during the decade. The most violent labor confrontations occurred in the mining and southern textile industries. The United Mine Workers of America, headed by John L. Lewis, was involved in bitter strikes in Pennsylvania, West Virginia, Kentucky, and Illinois, but by 1929 had lost most of its power. The United Textile Workers failed to organize southern textile workers in a campaign from 1927 to 1929, but violent strikes occurred in Tennessee, North Carolina, and Virginia.

5.1.9 *The Farm Problem*

Farmers did not share in the prosperity of the twenties. Farm prices had been high during World War I because of

European demand and government price fixing. By 1920 the European demand dropped considerably, and farm prices were determined by a free market. Farm income dropped from $10 billion annually in 1919 to about $4 billion in 1921, and then leveled off at about $7 billion a year from 1923 through 1929. During the same period farm expenses rose with the cost of more sophisticated machinery and a greater use of chemical fertilizers.

5.2 AMERICAN SOCIETY IN THE TWENTIES

5.2.1 *Population*

During the twenties the population of the United States increased by 16.1 percent from 105,710,620 in 1920 to 122,775,046 in 1930, a slower percentage of growth than in previous decades. The birthrate was also lower than in former times, dropping from 27.7 per 100,000 in 1920 to 21.3 per 100,000 in 1930. About 88 percent of the people were white.

5.2.2 *Urbanization*

In 1920 for the first time a majority of Americans, 51 percent, lived in an urban place with a population of 2,500 or more. By 1930 the figure had increased to 56 percent. In terms of Standard Metropolitan Areas, which are defined as areas with central cities of at least 50,000 population, 44 percent of the people lived in an SMA in 1920, and 50 percent in 1930. Farm residents dropped from 26 percent of the total population in 1920 to 21 percent in 1930. A new phenomenon of the twenties was the tremendous growth of suburbs and satellite cities, which grew more rapidly than the central cities. Streetcars, commuter railroads, and automobiles contributed to the process, as well as the easy availability of financing for home construction. The suburbs had once been the domain of the wealthy, but the technology of the twenties opened them to working-class families.

5.2.3   *The Standard of Living*

Improved technology and urbanization led to a sharp rise in the standard of living. Urban living improved access to electricity, natural gas, telephones, and piped water. Two-thirds of American homes had electricity by 1929. The use of indoor plumbing, hot water, and central heating increased dramatically. Conveniences such as electric stoves, vacuum cleaners, refrigerators, washing machines, toasters, and irons made life less burdensome. Improved machinery produced better-fitting and more comfortable ready-made clothing and shoes. Diet improved as the consumption of fresh vegetables increased 45 percent and canned vegetables 35 percent. Sales of citrus fruit and canned fruit were also up. Correspondingly, per capita consumption of wheat, corn, and potatoes fell. Automobiles, radios, phonographs, and commercial entertainment added to the enjoyment of life. Yet enjoyment of the new standard of living was uneven. The one-third of the households which still did not have electricity in 1929 lacked access to many of the new products. For those who had access, the new standard of living required more money than had been necessary in former times. Despite heavy sales of appliances, by 1929 only 25 percent of American families had vacuum cleaners, and only 20 percent had electric toasters. The real income of workers increased about 11 percent during the decade, but others suffered a decline in real income, including farmers who still comprised about one-fourth of the population. It is estimated that the bottom 93 percent of the population had an average increase in real income of six percent during the twenties. In 1929 about twelve million families, or 43 percent of the total, had annual incomes under $1,500, which was considered by many to be the poverty line. About twenty million families, or 72 percent, had incomes under $2,500, the family income deemed necessary for a decent standard of living with reasonable comforts.

5.2.4 *The Sexual Revolution*

Traditional American moral standards regarding premarital sex and marital fidelity were widely questioned for the first time during the twenties. There was a popular misunderstanding by people who had not read his works that Sigmund Freud had advocated sexual promiscuity. Movies, novels, and magazine stories were more sexually explicit and sensational. The "flaming youth" of the "Jazz Age" emphasized sexual promiscuity and drinking, as well as new forms of dancing considered erotic by the older generation. The automobile, by giving people mobility and privacy, was generally considered to have contributed to sexual license. Journalists wrote about "flappers," young women who were independent, assertive, and promiscuous. Birth control, though illegal, was promoted by Margaret Sanger and others, and was widely accepted. The sexual revolution occurred mostly among some urban dwellers, middle class people, and students, who were an economically-select group at the time. Many continued to adhere to the old ways. Compared with the period from 1960 to the present, it was a relatively conservative time.

5.2.5 *Women*

Many feminists believed that the passage of the Nineteenth Amendment in 1920 providing woman suffrage would solve all problems for women. When it became apparent that women did not vote as a block, political leaders gave little additional attention to the special concerns of women. The sexual revolution brought some emancipation. Women adopted less bulky clothing with short skirts and bare arms and necks. They could smoke and socialize with men in public more freely than before. Birth control was more acceptable. Divorce laws were liberalized in many states at the insistence of women. In 1920 there was 1 divorce for every 7.5 marriages. By 1929 the ratio was 1 in 6. The number of employed women rose from 8.4 million in 1920 to 10.6 million in 1929, but the total work force increased in about the same proportion. Black and foreign-born women comprised 57 percent of the female work force, and domestic service was the largest job category. Most other women workers were in traditional female occupations such as secretarial and clerical work, retail sales, teaching, and nursing. Rates of pay were below those for men. Most women still pursued the traditional role of housewife and mother, and society accepted that as the norm.

5.2.6 Blacks

The migration of southern rural blacks to the cities continued, with about 1.5 million moving during the twenties. By 1930 about 20 percent of American blacks lived in the North, with the largest concentrations in New York, Chicago, and Philadelphia. While they were generally better off economically in the cities than they had been as tenant farmers, they generally held low-paying jobs and were confined to segregated areas of the cities. The Harlem section of New York City, with a black population of 73,000 in 1920 and 165,000 in 1930, was the largest black urban community, and became the center for black writers, musicians, and intellectuals. Blacks throughout the country developed jazz and blues as music forms which enjoyed great popularity. W. E. B. DuBois, the editor of *The Crisis*, continued to call for integration and to attack segregation despite his disappointment with the lack of progress after World War I. The National Association for the Advancement of Colored People was a more conservative but active voice for civil rights, and the National Urban League concentrated on employment and economic advancement. Lynchings continued in the South, and the anti-black activities of the Ku Klux Klan will be mentioned under Social Conflicts below.

5.2.7 *Marcus Garvey and the UNIA*

A native of Jamaica, Marcus Garvey founded the Universal Negro Improvement Association there in 1914, and moved to New York in 1916. He advocated black racial pride and separatism rather than integration, and a return of blacks to Africa. Some of his ideas soon alienated the older black organizations. He developed a large following, especially among southern blacks, but his claim of six million members in 1923 may be inflated. An advocate of black economic self-sufficiency, he urged his followers to buy only from blacks, and founded a chain of businesses, including grocery stores, restaurants, and laundries. In 1921 he proclaimed himself the provisional president of an African empire, and sold stock in the Black Star Steamship Line which would take migrants to Africa. The line went bankrupt in 1923, Garvey was convicted and imprisoned for mail fraud in the sale of the line's stock, and then deported. His legacy was an emphasis on black pride and self-respect.

5.2.8 *Mexicans and Puerto Ricans*

Mexicans had long migrated to the southwestern part of the United States as agricultural laborers, but in the twenties they began to settle in cities such as Los Angeles, San Antonio, and Denver. Like other immigrants, they held low-paying jobs and lived in poor neighborhoods, called *barrios*. The twenties also saw the first large migration of Puerto Ricans to the mainland, mostly to New York City. There they were employed in manufacturing, in service industries such as restaurants, and in domestic work. They lived in barrios in Brooklyn and Manhattan.

5.2.9 Education

Free elementary education was available to most students in 1920, except for many black children. Growth of elementary schools in the twenties reflected population growth and the addition of kindergartens. High school education became more available, and the number of secondary school students doubled from 2.2 million in 1920 to 4.4 million in 1930. High school instruction shifted from an emphasis on college preparation to include vocational education, which was funded in part by the Smith-Hughes Act of 1917 which gave federal funds for agricultural and technical studies. There was also a substantial growth in enrollment in higher education from 600,000 in 1920 to 1.1 million in 1930.

5.2.10 Religion

Church and synagogue membership increased more rapidly than the population during the twenties despite much religious tension and conflict. Most Protestants had been divided north and south since before the Civil War. By the twenties, there was another major division between the modernists who accommodated their thinking with modern biblical criticism and evolution, and fundamentalists who stressed the literal truth of the Bible and creationism. There was also division on social issues such as support of labor. The only issue which united most Protestants, except Lutherans, was prohibition. The Roman Catholic Church and Jewish congregations were assimilating the large number of immigrants who had arrived prior to 1922. They also found themselves under attack from the Ku Klux Klan and the immigration restrictions.

5.2.11 Popular Culture

The trend whereby entertainment shifted from the home and small social groups to commercial profit-making activities had begun in the late nineteenth century and reached maturity in the twenties. Spending for entertainment in 1929 was $4.3 billion. The movies attracted the most consumer interest and generated the most money. Movie attendance averaged 40 million a week in 1922 and 90 million a week in 1929. Introduction of sound with *The Jazz Singer* in 1927 generated even more interest. Stars like Douglas Fairbanks, Gloria Swanson, Rudolph Valentino, Clara Bow, and Charlie Chaplin were tremendously popular. Americans spent ten times more on movies than on all sports, the next attraction in popularity. It was called the golden age of major-league baseball, with an attendance increase of over fifty percent during the decade. Millions followed the exploits of George Herman "Babe" Ruth and other stars. Boxing was popular, and made Jack Dempsey and others famous. College football began to attract attention with Knute Rockne coaching at Notre Dame and Harold "Red" Grange playing for the University of Illinois. When Grange signed with the Chicago Bears in 1926, professional football began to grow in popularity. Commercial radio began when station KDKA in Pittsburgh broadcasted the election results in November 1920. By 1929 over ten million families, over one-third of the total, had radios. National network broadcasting began when the National Broadcasting Company was organized in 1926, followed by the Columbia Broadcasting System in 1927. Radio was free entertainment, paid for by advertising. Despite the many new diversions, Americans continued to read, and millions of popular magazines were sold each week. Popular books of the period included the Tarzan series and Zane Grey's westerns, as well as literary works, some of which are mentioned below.

5.2.12 *Literary Trends*

Many talented writers of the twenties were disgusted with the hypocrisy and materialism of contemporary American society, and expressed their concern in their works. Often called the "Lost Generation," many of them, such as novelists Ernest Hemingway and F. Scott Fitzgerald and poets Ezra Pound and

T.S. Eliot, moved to Europe. Typical authors and works include Ernest Hemingway's *The Sun Also Rises* (1926) and *A Farewell to Arms* (1929); Sinclair Lewis' *Babbitt* (1922), *Arrowsmith* (1925), and *Elmer Gantry* (1927); F. Scott Fitzgerald's *The Great Gatsby* (1925) and *Tender Is the Night* (1934); John Dos Passos' *Three Soldiers* (1921); and Thomas Wolfe's *Look Homeward, Angel* (1929). H. L. Mencken, a journalist who began publication of the *American Mercury* magazine in 1922, ceaselessly and vitriolicly attacked the "booboisie," as he called middle-class America, but his literary talent did not match that of the leaders of the period.

5.3   SOCIAL CONFLICTS

5.3.1   *A Conflict of Values*

The rapid technological changes represented by the automobile, the revolution in morals, and the rapid urbanization with many immigrants and blacks inhabiting the growing cities brought a strong reaction from white Protestant Americans of older stock who saw their traditional values gravely threatened. In many ways their concerns continued the emotions of wartime hysteria and the Red Scare. The traditionalists were largely residents of rural areas and small towns, and the clash of farm values with those of an industrial society of urban workers was evident. The conflict is often called a rural-urban conflict, and to a great extent it was, but some think the lines of division were not that neat. The traditionalist backlash against modern urban industrial society expressed itself primarily through intolerance.

5.3.2   *The Ku Klux Klan*

On Thanksgiving Day in 1915 the Knights of the Ku Klux Klan, modeled on the organization of the same name in the

1860s and 1870s, was founded near Atlanta by William J. Simmons. Its purpose was to intimidate blacks who were experiencing an apparent rise in status during World War I. The Klan remained small until 1920 when two advertising experts, Edward Y. Clark and Elizabeth Tyler, were hired by the leadership. Clark and Tyler used modern advertising to recruit members, charged a ten dollar initiation fee of which they received $2.50, and made additional money from the sale of regalia and emblems. By 1923 the Klan had about five million members throughout the nation. The largest concentrations of members were in the South, the Southwest, the Midwest, California, and Oregon. The use of white hoods, masks, and robes, and the secret ritual and jargon, seemed to appeal mostly to lower middle class men in towns and small cities. The Klan stood for "100 percent pure Americanism" to preserve "native, white, Protestant supremacy." It opposed blacks and Catholics primarily. In addition, Jews, Mexicans, Orientals, and foreigners were often its targets. It also attacked bootleggers, drunkards, gamblers, and adulterers for violating moral standards. The Klan's methods of repression included cross burnings, tar and featherings, kidnappings, lynchings, and burnings. The Klan was not a political party, but it endorsed and opposed candidates, and exerted considerable control over elections and politicians in at least nine states. The Klan began to decline after 1925 when it was hit by scandals, especially the murder conviction of Indiana Grand Dragon David Stephenson. The main reason for its decline was the staunch opposition of courageous editors, politicians, and other public figures who exposed its lawlessness and terrorism in the face of great personal danger of violence. Many historians see the Klan as the American expression of fascism which was making headway in Italy, Germany, and other European nations during the twenties.

5.3.3 *Immigration Restriction*

There had been calls for immigration restriction since the late nineteenth century. Labor leaders believed that immigrants depressed wages and impeded unionization. Some progressives believed that they created social problems. In June 1917 Congress, over Wilson's veto, had imposed a literacy test for immigrants and excluded many Asian nationalities. During World War I and the Red Scare, almost all immigrants were considered radicals and communists, and the tradition was quickly picked up by the Klan. With bad economic conditions in postwar Europe, over 1.3 million came to the United States during the three years from 1919 through 1921. As in the period before the war, they were mostly from south and east Europe and mostly Catholics and Jews, the groups most despised by nativist Americans. In 1921 Congress quickly passed the Emergency Quota Act which limited immigration by nation to three percent of the number of foreign-born persons from that nation in the United States in 1910. In practice, the law admitted about as many as wanted to come from such nations as Britain, Ireland, and Germany, while severely restricting Italians, Greeks, Poles, and east European Jews. It became effective in 1922 and reduced the number of immigrants annually to about forty percent of the 1921 total. Congress then passed the National Origins Act of 1924 which set the quotas at two percent of the number of foreign-born persons of that nationality in the United States in 1890, excluded all Orientals, and imposed an annual maximum of 164,000.

Immigration from western hemisphere nations, including Canada and Mexico, was not limited. The law further reduced the number of south and east Europeans, and cut the annual immigration to twenty percent of the 1921 figure. In 1927 the annual maximum was reduced to 150,000. The quotas were not fully calculated and implemented until 1929. Objections to the law were not aimed at the idea of restriction, but at the designation of certain nationalities and religious groups as undesirable. The law was resented by such groups as Italian-Americans and Polish-Americans.

5.3.4 *Prohibition*

The Eighteenth Amendment which prohibited the manufacture, sale, or transportation of intoxicating liquors took effect in January 1920. It was implemented by the Volstead Act of October 1919 which defined intoxicating beverages as containing one-half of one percent alcohol by volume and imposed criminal penalties for violations. Many states had authorized the sale of light beer, believing that it was not covered by the amendment, but Anti-Saloon League lobbyists pushed through the Volstead Act. Many historians believe that prohibition of hard liquor might have been successful if light wine and beer had been allowed. As things turned out, the inexpensive light beverages were less available while expensive illegal hard liquor was readily available. Prohibition was enforceable only if many people in the society accepted and supported it. Enforcement was reasonably effective in some rural southern and midwestern states which had been dry before the amendment. In urban areas where both foreign-born and native citizens often believed that their liberty had been infringed upon, neither the public nor their elected officials were interested in enforcement. Speakeasies, supposedly secret bars operated by bootleggers, replaced the saloons. Smuggled liquor flowed across the boundaries and coastlines of the nation, and the manufacture of "bathtub gin" and similar beverages was undertaken by thousands. Organized crime, which previously had been involved mainly with prostitution and gambling, grew tremendously to meet the demand. Al Capone of Chicago was perhaps the most famous of the bootlegging gangsters. The automobile was used both to transport liquor and to take customers to speakeasies. Women, who had not gone to saloons in the pre-prohibition period, frequented speakeasies and began to drink in public. By the mid-twenties, the nation was badly divided on the prohibition issue. Support continued from rural areas and almost all Republican office-holders. The Democrats divided between the urban northerners who advocated repeal, and rural, especially southern, Democrats who supported prohibition. Some people who originally favored prohibition changed their views because of the public hypocrisy and criminal activity which it caused.

5.3.5 *Creationism and the Scopes Trial*

Fundamentalist Protestants, under the leadership of William Jennings Bryan, began a campaign in 1921 to prohibit the teaching of evolution in the schools, and thus protect belief in the literal Biblical account of creation. The idea was especially well-received in the South. In 1925 the Tennessee legislature passed a law which forbade any teacher in the state's schools or colleges to teach evolution. The American Civil Liberties Union found a young high school biology teacher, John Thomas Scopes, who was willing to bring about a test case by breaking the law. Scopes was tried in Dayton, Tennessee, in July 1925. Bryan came to assist the prosecution, and Chicago trial lawyer Clarence Darrow defended Scopes. The trial attracted national attention through newspaper and radio coverage. The judge refused to allow expert testimony, so the trial was a duel of words between Darrow and Bryan. As was expected, Scopes was convicted and fined one hundred dollars. Bryan died of exhaustion a few days after the trial. Both sides claimed a moral victory. The anti-evolution crusaders continued their efforts, and secured enactment of a statute in Mississippi in 1926. They failed after a bitter fight in North Carolina in 1927, and in several other states until Arkansas in 1928 passed an anti-evolution law by use of the initiative.

5.3.6 *Sacco and Vanzetti*

On April 15, 1920 two unidentified gunmen robbed a shoe factory and killed two men in South Braintree, Massachusetts. Nicola Sacco and Bartolomeo Vanzetti, Italian immigrants and admitted anarchists, were tried for murder. Judge Webster Thayer clearly favored the prosecution, which based its case on the political radicalism of the defendants. After they were convicted and sentenced to death in July 1921, there was much protest in the United States and in Europe that they had not received a fair trial. After six years of delays, they were executed on August 23, 1927. A debate on their innocence and the possible perversion of American justice has continued until the present.

CHAPTER 6

GOVERNMENT AND POLITICS IN THE TWENTIES

6.1 THE HARDING ADMINISTRATION

6.1.1 *Warren G. Harding*

Harding was a handsome and amiable man of limited intellectual and organizational abilities. He had spent much of his life as the publisher of a newspaper in the small city of Marion, Ohio. He recognized his limitations, but hoped to be a much-loved president. He showed compassion by pardoning socialist Eugene V. Debs for his conviction under the Espionage Act and inviting him to dinner at the White House. He also persuaded U.S. Steel to give workers the eight-hour day. A convivial man, he liked to drink and play poker with his friends, and kept the White House stocked with bootleg liquor despite prohibition. He was accused of keeping a mistress, Nan Britton. His economic philosophy was conservative.

6.1.2 *The Cabinet and Government Appointments*

Harding appointed some outstanding persons to his cabinet, including Secretary of State Charles Evans Hughes, a former

Supreme Court justice and presidential candidate; Secretary of the Treasury Andrew Mellon, a Pittsburgh aluminum and banking magnate and reportedly the richest man in America; and Secretary of Commerce Herbert Hoover, a dynamic multimillionaire mine owner and famous for wartime relief efforts. Less impressive was his appointment of his cronies Albert B. Fall as secretary of the interior and Harry M. Daugherty as attorney general. Other cronies, some dishonest, were appointed to other government posts.

6.1.3 Tax Reduction

Mellon believed in low taxes and government economy to free the rich from "oppressive" taxes and thus encourage investment. The farm bloc of midwestern Republicans and southern Democrats in Congress prevented cuts in the higher tax brackets as great as Mellon recommended. The Revenue Acts of 1921 and 1924 cut the maximum tax rates to fifty percent and then to forty percent. Taxes in lower brackets were also reduced, but inheritance and corporate income taxes were retained. Despite the cuts, Mellon was able to reduce the federal debt by an average of $500 million a year.

6.1.4 The Fordney-McCumber Tariff

Mellon sought substantial increases in the tariffs, but again there was a compromise with the farm bloc. The Fordney-McCumber Tariff of September 1922 imposed high rates on farm products and protected such infant industries as rayon, china, toys, and chemicals. Most other items received moderate protection, and a few items including farm equipment, were duty-free. The president could raise or lower rates to a limit of fifty percent on recommendation of the Tariff Commission. The average rate was about 33 percent, compared with about 26 percent under the previous tariff.

6.1.5 *The Budget*

As a result of the Budget and Accounting Act of 1921, the federal government had a unified budget for the first time. The law also provided for a director of the budget to assist in its preparation, and a comptroller general to audit government accounts.

6.1.6 *The Harding Scandals*

Harding apparently was completely honest, but several of his friends whom he appointed to office became involved in major financial scandals. Most of the information about the scandals did not become public knowledge until after Harding's death. Three of the more famous scandals were as follows:

1) *The Teapot Dome Scandal.* Secretary of the Interior Albert B. Fall in 1921 secured the transfer of several naval oil reserves to his jurisdiction. In 1922 he secretly leased reserves at Teapot Dome in Wyoming to Harry F. Sinclair of Monmouth Oil and at Elk Hills in California to Edward Doheny of Pan-American Petroleum. A Senate investigation later revealed that Sinclair had given Fall $305,000 in cash and bonds and a herd of cattle, while Doheny had given him a $100,000 unsecured loan. Sinclair and Doheny were acquitted in 1927 of charges of defrauding the government, but in 1929 Fall was convicted, fined, and imprisoned for bribery.

2) *The Veterans' Bureau.* Charles R. Forbes, appointed by Harding to head the new Veterans' Bureau, seemed energetic and efficient in operating the new hospitals and services for veterans. It was later estimated that he had stolen or squandered about $250 million in bureau funds.

3) *Attorney General Daugherty.* The attorney general, through his intimate friend Jesse Smith, took bribes from bootleggers, income tax evaders, and others in return for protection from prosecution. When the scandal began to come to light, Smith committed suicide in Daugherty's Washington apartment in May 1923. There was also evidence that Daugherty received money for using his influence in returning the American Metal Company, seized by the government during the war, to its German owners.

6.1.7 Harding's Death

Depressed by the first news of the scandals, Harding left in June 1923 for an extended trip including a tour of Alaska. On his return to California, he died suddenly in San Francisco on August 2, 1923, apparently of a heart attack. Rumors of foul play or suicide persisted for years.

6.1.8 Coolidge Becomes President

Vice President Calvin Coolidge became president to complete Harding's term. As the scandals of the deceased president's administration came to light, Coolidge was able to avoid responsibility for them. He had a reputation for honesty, although he did not remove Daugherty from the cabinet until March 1924.

6.2 THE ELECTION OF 1924

6.2.1 The Republicans

Progressive insurgents failed to capture the convention. Calvin Coolidge was nominated on the first ballot with Charles G. Dawes as his running mate. The platform endorsed business development, low taxes, and rigid economy in government. The party stood on its record of economic growth and prosperity since 1922.

6.2.2 The Democrats

The party had an opportunity to draw farmers and labor into a new progressive coalition. An attractive Democratic candidate would have had a good chance against the bland Coolidge and the Harding scandals. Instead, two wings of the party battled to exhaustion at the convention. The eastern wing, led by Governor Alfred E. Smith of New York, wanted the platform to favor repeal of prohibition and to condemn the Ku Klux Klan. Southern and western delegates, led by William G. McAdoo and William Jennings Bryan, narrowly defeated both proposals. Smith and McAdoo contested for 103 ballots with neither receiving the two-thirds necessary for nomination. John W. Davis, a conservative Wall Street lawyer, was finally chosen as a dark horse with Charles W. Bryan, brother of William Jennings, as the vice presidential candidate. The platform favored a lower tariff, but otherwise was similar to the Republican document.

6.2.3 The Progressives

Robert M. LaFollette, after failing in a bid for the Republican nomination, formed a new Progressive Party with support from midwest farm groups, socialists, and the American Federation of Labor. The platform attacked monopolies, and called for the nationalization of railroads, the direct election of the president, and other reforms.

6.2.4 The Campaign

Neither Coolidge nor Davis were active or effective campaigners. Republican publicity concentrated on attacking

LaFollette as a communist. LaFollette campaigned vigorously, but he lacked money and was disliked by many for his 1917 opposition to entrance into World War I.

6.2.5 The Election

Coolidge received 15,725,016 votes and 382 electoral votes, more than his two opponents combined. Davis received 8,385,586 votes and 136 electoral votes, while LaFollette had 4,822,856 votes and 36 electoral votes from his home state of Wisconsin.

6.3 THE COOLIDGE ADMINISTRATION

6.3.1 Calvin Coolidge

Coolidge was a dour and taciturn man. Born in Vermont, his adult life and political career were spent in Massachusetts. "The business of the United States is business," he proclaimed, and "the man who builds a factory builds a temple." His philosophy of life was stated in the remark that "four-fifths of all our troubles in this world would disappear if only we would sit down and keep still." Liberal political commentator Walter Lippmann wrote that "Mr. Coolidge's genius for inactivity is developed to a very high point." He intentionally provided no presidential leadership.

6.3.2 The McNary-Haugen Bill

In 1921 George Peek and Hugh S. Johnson, farm machinery manufacturers in Illinois, developed a plan to raise prices for basic farm products. The government would buy and resell in the domestic market a commodity such as wheat at the world price plus the tariff. The surplus would be sold abroad at the world price, and the difference made up by an equalization fee on all farmers in proportion to the amount of the commodity they had sold. When farm conditions did not improve, the idea was incorporated in the McNary-Haugen bill which passed Congress in 1927 and 1928, but was vetoed both times by Coolidge. The plan was a forerunner of the agricultural programs of the thirties.

6.3.3 *Muscle Shoals*

During World War I the government had constructed a dam and two nitrate plants on the Tennessee River at Muscle Shoals, Alabama. In 1925 Senator George W. Norris of Nebraska led the defeat of a plan to lease the property to private business, but his proposal for government operation was vetoed by Coolidge in 1928. The facility was to become the nucleus of the Tennessee Valley Authority in the thirties.

6.3.4 *Veterans' Bonus*

Legislation to give veterans of World War I twenty-year endowment policies with values based on their length of service was passed over Coolidge's veto in 1924.

6.3.5 *The Revenue Act of 1926*

Mellon's tax policies were finally implemented by this law which reduced the basic income tax, cut the surtax to a maximum of twenty percent, abolished the gift tax, and cut the estate tax in half.

6.4 THE ELECTION OF 1928

6.4.1 *The Republicans*

Coolidge did not seek another term, and the convention quickly nominated Herbert Hoover, the secretary of commerce, for president, and Charles Curtis as his running mate. The platform endorsed the policies of the Harding and Coolidge administrations.

6.4.2 *The Democrats*

Governor Alfred E. Smith of New York, a Catholic and an anti-prohibitionist, controlled most of the non-southern delegations. Southerners supported his nomination with the understanding that the platform would not advocate repeal of prohibition. Senator Joseph T. Robinson of Arkansas, a Protestant and a prohibitionist, was the vice presidential candidate. The platform differed little from the Republican, except in advocating lower tariffs.

6.4.3 *The Campaign*

Hoover asserted that Republican policies would end poverty in the country. Smith was also economically conservative, but he attacked prohibition and bigotry. He was met in the South by a massive campaign headed by Bishop James Cannon, Jr., of the Methodist Episcopal Church South, attacking him as a Catholic and a wet.

6.4.4 *The Election*

Hoover received 21,392,190 votes and 444 electoral votes, carrying all of the North except Massachusetts and Rhode Island, and seven states in the Solid South. Smith had 15,016,443 votes for 87 electoral votes in eight states.

6.5 FOREIGN POLICY IN THE TWENTIES

6.5.1 *The Washington Conference*

At the invitation of Secretary of State Charles Evans Hughes, representatives of the United States, Great Britain, France, Japan, Italy, China, the Netherlands, Belgium, and Portugal met in Washington in August 1921 to discuss naval limitations and Asian affairs. Three treaties resulted from the conference:

1) *The Five Power Pact* or *Treaty*, signed in February 1922, committed the United States, Britain, Japan, France, and Italy to end new construction of capital naval vessels, to scrap some ships, and to maintain a ratio of 5:5:3:1.67:1.67 for tonnage of capital or major ships in order of the nations listed. Hughes did not realize that the treaty gave Japan naval supremacy in the Pacific.

2) *The Nine Power Pact* or *Treaty* was signed by all of the participants at the conference. It upheld the Open Door in China by binding the nations to respect the sovereignty, independence, and integrity of China.

3) *The Four Power Pact* or *Treaty* bound the United States, Great Britain, Japan, and France to respect each other's possessions in the Pacific, and to confer in the event of disputes or aggression in the area.

6.5.2 *War Debts, Reparations, and International Finance*

The United States had loaned the Allies about $7 billion during World War I and about $3.25 billion in the postwar period, and insisted on full payment of the debts. Meanwhile, Germany was to pay reparations to the Allies, but by 1923 Germany was bankrupt. The Dawes Plan, proposed by American banker Charles G. Dawes, was accepted in 1924. Under it, American banks made loans of $2.5 billion to Germany by 1930. Germany paid reparations of over $2 billion to the Allies during the same period, and the Allies paid about $2.6 billion to the United States on their war debts. The whole cycle was based on loans from American banks.

6.5.3 The Kellogg-Briand Pact

A group of American citizens campaigned during the twenties for a treaty which would outlaw war. In 1927 the French foreign minister, Aristide Briand, proposed such a treaty with the United States. Frank B. Kellogg, Coolidge's secretary of state, countered by proposing that other nations be invited to sign. At Paris in August 1928 almost all major nations signed the treaty which renounced war as an instrument of national policy. It outlawed only aggression, not self-defense, and had no enforcement provisions.

6.5.4 Latin America

American investment in Latin America almost doubled during the twenties to $5.4 billion, and relations with most nations in the region improved. Coolidge removed the marines from Nicaragua in 1925, but a revolution erupted and the marines were returned. Revolutionary General Augusto Sandino fought against the marines until they were replaced by an American-trained national guard under Anastasio Somoza. The Somoza family ruled Nicaragua until 1979 when they were overthrown by revolutionaries called the Sandinistas.

CHAPTER 7

THE GREAT DEPRESSION

7.1 THE CRASH

7.1.1 *Hoover Becomes President*

Herbert Hoover, an Iowa farm boy and an orphan, graduated from Stanford University with a degree in mining engineering. He became a multimillionaire from mining and other investments around the world. After serving as the director of the Food Administration under Wilson, he became secretary of commerce under Harding and Coolidge. He believed that an associative economic system with voluntary cooperation of business and government would enable the United States to abolish poverty through continued economic growth.

7.1.2 *The Stock Market Boom*

Stock prices increased throughout the twenties. The boom in prices and volume of sales was especially active after 1925, and was intensive during 1928 and 1929. The Dow-Jones Industrial Average for the year 1924 was 120; for the month of September 1929 it was 381; and for the year 1932 it dropped to

41. Stocks were selling for more than sixteen times their earnings in 1929, well above the rule of thumb of ten times their earnings.

7.1.3 The Stock Market Crash

Careful investors, realizing that stocks were overpriced, began to sell to take their profits. During October 1929 prices declined as more stock was sold. On "Black Thursday," October 24, 1929, almost thirteen million shares were traded, a large number for that time, and prices fell precipitously. Investment banks tried to boost the market by buying, but on October 29, "Black Tuesday," the market fell about forty points with 16.5 million shares traded. A long decline followed until early 1933, and with it, depression.

7.1.4 Other Reasons for the Depression

A stock market crash does not mean that a depression must follow. A similar crash in October 1987 did not lead to depression. In 1929 a complex interaction of many factors caused the decline of the economy:

1) Many people had bought stock on a margin of ten percent, meaning that they had borrowed ninety percent of the purchase through a broker's loan, and put up the stock as collateral. Broker's loans totaled $8.5 billion in 1929, compared with $3.5 billion in 1926. When the price of a stock fell more than ten percent, the lender sold the stock for whatever it would bring and thus further depressed prices. The forced sales brought great losses to the banks and businesses which had financed the broker's loans, as well as to the investors.

2) There were already signs of recession before the market crash in 1929. Because the gathering and processing of

statistics was not as advanced then as now, some factors were not so obvious to people at the time. The farm economy, which involved almost twenty-five percent of the population, had been depressed throughout the decade. Coal, railroads, and New England textiles had not been prosperous. After 1927 new construction declined and auto sales began to sag. Many workers had been laid off before the crash of 1929.

3) Many scholars believe that there was a problem of underconsumption, meaning that ordinary workers and farmers, after using their consumer credit, did not have enough money to keep buying the products which were being produced. One estimate says that the income of the top one percent of the population increased at least 75 percent during the decade, while that of the bottom 93 percent increased only 6 percent. The process continued after the depression began. After the stock market crash, people were conservative and saved their money, thus reducing the demand for goods. As demand decreased, workers were laid off or had wage reductions, further reducing their purchasing power and bringing another decrease in demand.

4) With the decline in the economy, Americans had less money for foreign loans and bought fewer imported products. That meant that foreign governments and individuals were not able to pay their debts in the United States. The whole reparations and war debts structure described in Chapter 6.5 collapsed. American exports dropped, further hurting the domestic economy. The depression eventually spread throughout the world.

7.1.5 *Economic Effects of the Depression*

During the early months of the depression most people

BANKS GOING BANKRUPT

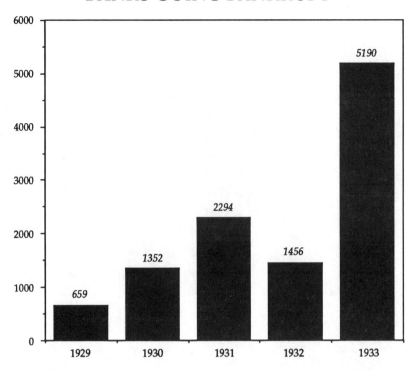

thought it was just an adjustment in the business cycle which would soon be over. Hoover repeatedly assured the public that prosperity was just around the corner. As time went on, the worst depression in American history set in, reaching its bottom point in early 1932. The gross national product fell from $104.6 billion in 1929 to $56.1 billion in 1933. Unemployment reached about 13 million in 1933, or about 25 percent of the labor force excluding farmers. National income dropped 54 percent from $87.8 billion to $40.2 billion. Labor income fell about 41 percent, while farm income dropped 55 percent from $11.9 billion to $5.3 billion. Industrial production dropped about 51 percent. The banking system suffered as 5,761 banks, over 22 percent of the total, failed by the end of 1932.

UNEMPLOYMENT, 1929 – 1945

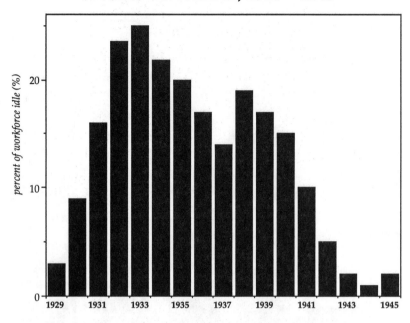

7.1.6   *The Human Dimension of the Depression*

As the depression grew worse, more and more people lost their jobs or had their wages reduced. Many were unable to continue credit payments on homes, automobiles, and other possessions, and lost them. Families doubled up in houses and apartments. Both the marriage rate and the birth rate declined as people put off family formation. Hundreds of thousands became homeless and lived in groups of makeshift shacks called Hoovervilles in empty spaces around cities. Others traveled the country by foot and boxcar seeking food and work. State and local government agencies and private charities were overwhelmed in their attempts to care for those in need, although public and private soup kitchens and bread lines were set up throughout the nation. Malnutrition was widespread but few died of starvation, perhaps because malnourished people are susceptible to many fatal diseases.

7.2 HOOVER'S DEPRESSION POLICIES

7.2.1 *The Agricultural Marketing Act*

Passed in June 1929 before the market crash, this law proposed by the president created the Federal Farm Board with a revolving fund of $500 million to lend to agricultural cooperatives to buy commodities such as wheat and cotton, and hold them for higher prices. Until 1931 it did keep agricultural prices above the world level. Then world prices plummeted, the board's funds ran out, and there was no period of higher prices in which the cooperatives could sell their stored commodities.

7.2.2 *The Hawley-Smoot Tariff*

This law, passed in June 1930, raised duties on both agricultural and manufactured imports. It did nothing of significance to improve the economy, and historians argue over whether or not it contributed to the spread of the international depression.

7.2.3 *Voluntarism*

Hoover believed that voluntary cooperation would enable the country to weather the depression. He held meetings with business leaders at which he urged them to avoid lay-offs of workers and wage cuts, and he secured no-strike pledges from labor leaders. He urged all citizens to contribute to charities to help alleviate the suffering. While people were generous, private charity could not begin to meet the needs.

7.2.4 *Public Works*

In 1930 Congress appropriated $750 million for public buildings, river and harbor improvements, and highway construction in an effort to stimulate employment.

7.2.5 *The Reconstruction Finance Corporation*

Chartered by Congress in 1932, the RFC had an appropriation of $500 million and authority to borrow $1.5 billion for loans to railroads, banks, and other financial institutions. It prevented the failure of basic firms on which many other elements of the economy depended, but was criticized by some as relief for the rich.

7.2.6 *The Federal Home Loan Bank Act*

This law, passed in July 1932, created home loan banks with a capital of $125 million to make loans to building and loan associations, savings banks, and insurance companies to help them avoid foreclosures on homes.

7.2.7 *Relief*

Hoover staunchly opposed the use of federal funds for relief for the needy. In July 1932 he vetoed the Garner-Wagner Bill which would have appropriated funds for relief. He did compromise by approving legislation authorizing the RFC to lend $300 million to the states for relief, and to make loans to states and cities for self-liquidating public works.

7.2.8 *The Bonus Army*

The Bonus Expeditionary Force, which took its name from the American Expeditionary Force of World War I, was a group of about fourteen thousand unemployed veterans who went to Washington in the summer of 1932 to lobby Congress for immediate payment of the bonus which had been approved in 1924 for payment in 1945. At Hoover's insistence, the Senate did not pass the bonus bill, and about half of the BEF accepted a Congressional offer of transportation home. The remaining five or six thousand, many with wives and children, continued to live in shanties along the Anacostia river and to lobby for their cause. After two veterans were killed in a clash with the police, Hoover, calling them insurrectionists and communists, ordered the army to remove them. On July 28, 1932 General Douglas MacArthur, the army chief of staff, assisted by Majors Dwight D. Eisenhower and George S. Patton, personally commanded the removal operation. With machine guns, tanks, cavalry, infantry with fixed bayonets, and tear gas, MacArthur drove the veterans from Washington and burned their camp.

7.2.9 *The Farm Holiday Association*

Centered in Iowa, the association, headed by Milo Reno and others, called a farm strike in August 1932. They urged farmers not to take their products to market in an effort to raise farm prices. The picketing of markets led to violence, and the strike collapsed.

7.3 THE ELECTION OF 1932

7.3.1 *The Republicans*

At the convention in Chicago Hoover was nominated on the first ballot. The platform called for a continuation of his depression policies.

7.3.2 *The Democrats*

Franklin D. Roosevelt, the popular governor of New York, gained the support of many southern and western delegates through the efforts of his managers, Louis Howe and James Farley. When the convention opened in Chicago, he had a majority of delegates, but not the necessary two-thirds for nomination. House Speaker John Nance Garner, a favorite son candidate from Texas, threw support to Roosevelt, who was nominated on the fourth ballot. Garner then became the vice presidential candidate. Roosevelt took the unprecedented step of flying to the convention to accept the nomination in person, declaring that he pledged a "new deal" for the American people. The platform called for the repeal of prohibition, government aid for the unemployed, and a twenty-five percent cut in government spending.

7.3.3 *The Campaign*

Hoover declared that he would lead the nation to prosperity with higher tariffs and the maintenance of the gold standard. He warned that the election of Roosevelt would lead to grass growing in the streets of the cities and towns of America. Roosevelt called for "bold, persistent experimentation," and expressed his concern for the "forgotten man" at the bottom of the economic heap, but he did not give a clear picture of what he intended to do. Roosevelt had a broad smile and amiable disposition which attracted many people, while Hoover was aloof and cold in his personal style.

7.3.4 *The Election*

Roosevelt received 22,809,638 votes for 57.3 percent of the total, and 472 electoral votes, carrying all but six northeastern states. Hoover had 15,758,901 votes and 59 electoral votes. Despite the hard times, Norman Thomas, the Socialist candidate, received only 881,951 votes. The Democrats also captured the Senate, and increased their majority in the House.

CHAPTER 8

THE FIRST NEW DEAL

8.1 THE ROOSEVELT ADMINISTRATION BEGINS

8.1.1 *Franklin D. Roosevelt*

The heir of a wealthy family and a fifth cousin of Theodore Roosevelt, Franklin was born in 1882 on the family estate at Hyde Park, New York, graduated from Harvard and the Columbia Law School, married his distant cousin Anna Eleanor Roosevelt in 1905, and practiced law in New York City. He entered state politics, then served as assistant secretary of the navy under Wilson, and was the Democratic vice presidential candidate in 1920. In 1921 he suffered an attack of polio which left him paralyzed for several years and on crutches or in a wheelchair for the rest of his life. In 1928 he was elected governor of New York to succeed Al Smith, and was reelected in 1930. As governor, his depression programs for the unemployed, public works, aid to farmers, and conservation attracted national attention.

8.1.2 *The Cabinet*

Important cabinet appointments included Senator Cordell Hull of Tennessee as secretary of state; Henry A. Wallace as secretary of agriculture; Harold L. Ickes as secretary of the interior; Frances Perkins, a New York social worker, as secretary of labor and the first woman appointed to a cabinet post; and James A. Farley, Roosevelt's political manager, as postmaster general.

8.1.3 *The Brain Trust*

Roosevelt's inner circle of unofficial advisers, first assembled during the campaign, was more influential than the cabinet. Prominent in it were agricultural economist Rexford G. Tugwell, political scientist Raymond Moley, lawyer Adolph A. Berle, Jr., the originators of the McNary-Haugen Bill – Hugh S. Johnson and George Peek – and Roosevelt's personal political advisor, Louis Howe.

8.1.4 *The New Deal Program*

Roosevelt did not have a developed plan of action when he took office. He intended to experiment and to find that which worked. As a result, many programs overlapped or contradicted others, and were changed or dropped if they did not work.

8.1.5 *Repeal of Prohibition*

In February 1933, before Roosevelt took office, Congress passed the Twenty-first Amendment to repeal prohibition, and sent it to the states. In March the new Congress legalized light beer. The amendment was ratified by the states and took effect in December 1933.

8.1.6 *The Banking Crisis*

In February 1933, as the inauguration approached, a severe banking crisis developed. Banks could not collect their loans or meet the demands of their depositors for withdrawals, and runs occurred on many banks. Eventually banks in thirty-eight states were closed by the state governments, and the remainder were open for only limited operations. An additional 5,190 banks failed in 1933, bringing the depression total to 10,951.

8.1.7 *The Inaugural Address*

When Roosevelt was inaugurated on March 4, 1933, the American economic system seemed to be on the verge of collapse. Roosevelt assured the nation that "the only thing we have to fear is fear itself," called for a special session of Congress to convene on March 9, and asked for "broad executive powers to wage war against the emergency." Two days later, he closed all banks, and forbade the export of gold or the redemption of currency in gold.

8.2 LEGISLATION OF THE FIRST NEW DEAL

8.2.1 *The Hundred Days and the First New Deal*

The special session of Congress, from March 9 to June 16, 1933, passed a great body of legislation which has left a lasting mark on the nation, and the period has been referred to ever since as the "Hundred Days." Over the next two years legislation was added, but the basic recovery plan of the Hundred Days remained in operation. Hence, the period from 1933 to 1935 is called the First New Deal. A new wave of programs beginning in 1935 is called the Second New Deal. The distinction was not known at the time, but is a device of historians to differentiate between two stages in Roosevelt's administration.

8.2.2 Economic Legislation of the Hundred Days

The banking crisis was the most immediate problem facing Roosevelt and the Congress. A series of laws were passed to deal with the crisis and to reform the American economic system:

1) *Emergency Banking Relief Act* was passed on March 9, the first day of the special session. The law provided additional funds for banks from the RFC and the Federal Reserve, allowed the Treasury to open sound banks after ten days and to merge or liquidate unsound ones, and forbade the hoarding or export of gold. Roosevelt on March 12 assured the public of the soundness of the banks in the first of many "fireside chats," or radio addresses. People believed him and most banks were soon open with more deposits than withdrawals.

2) *The Banking Act of 1933,* or the Glass-Steagall Act, established the Federal Deposit Insurance Corporation (FDIC) to insure individual deposits in commercial banks, and separated commercial banking from the more speculative activity of investment banking.

3) *The Truth-in-Securities Act* required that full information about stocks and bonds be provided by brokers and others to potential purchasers.

4) *The Home Owners Loan Corporation (HOLC)* had authority to borrow money to refinance home mortgages and thus prevent foreclosures. Eventually it lent over three billion dollars to over one million home owners.

5) Gold was taken out of circulation following the president's order of March 6, and the nation went off the gold standard. Eventually, on January 31, 1934, the value of the dollar was set at $35 per ounce of gold, 59 percent of its former value. The object of the devaluation was to raise prices and help American exports.

8.2.3 Later Economic Legislation of the First New Deal

The *Securities and Exchange Commission* was created in 1934 to supervise stock exchanges and to punish fraud in securities trading.

The *Federal Housing Administration (FHA)* was created by Congress in 1934 to insure long-term, low-interest mortgages for home construction and repair.

8.2.4 Relief and Employment Programs of the Hundred Days

These programs were intended to provide temporary relief for people in need, and to be disbanded when the economy improved:

1) *The Federal Emergency Relief Act* appropriated $500 million for aid to the poor to be distributed by state and local governments. Half of the funds were to be distributed on a one to three matching basis with the states. It also established the Federal Emergency Relief Administration under Harry Hopkins. Additional appropriations were made many times later.

2) *The Civilian Conservation Corps* enrolled 250,000 young men ages 18 to 24 from families on relief to go to camps where they worked on flood control, soil con-

servation, and forest projects under the direction of the War Department. A small monthly payment was made to the family of each member. By the end of the decade, 2.75 million young men had served in the corps.

3) *The Public Works Administration,* under Secretary of the Interior Harold Ickes, had $3.3 billion to distribute to state and local governments for building projects such as schools, highways, and hospitals. The object was to "prime the pump" of the economy by creating construction jobs. Additional money was appropriated later.

8.2.5　*Later Relief Efforts*

After the Hundred Days, in November 1933, Roosevelt established the Civil Works Administration under Harry Hopkins with $400 million from the Public Works Administration to hire four million unemployed workers. The temporary and makeshift nature of the jobs, such as sweeping streets, brought much criticism, and the experiment was terminated in April 1934.

8.2.6　*Agricultural Programs of the Hundred Days*

The Agricultural Adjustment Act of 1933 created the Agricultural Adjustment Administration (AAA) which was headed by George Peek. It sought to return farm prices to parity with those of the 1909 to 1914 period. Farmers agreed to reduce production of principal farm commodities and were paid a subsidy in return. The money came from a tax on the processing of the commodities. Farm prices increased, but tenants and sharecroppers were hurt when owners took land out of cultivation. The law was declared unconstitutional in January 1936 on the grounds that the processing tax was not constitutional.

The Federal Farm Loan Act consolidated all farm credit programs into the Farm Credit Administration to make low-interest loans for farm mortgages and other agricultural purposes.

8.2.7 Later Agricultural Programs

The Commodity Credit Corporation was established in October 1933 by the AAA to make loans to corn and cotton farmers against their crops so that they could hold them for higher prices.

The Frazier-Lemke Farm Bankruptcy Act of 1934 allowed farmers to defer foreclosure on their land while they obtained new financing, and helped them to recover property already lost through easy financing.

8.2.8 The National Industrial Recovery Act

This law, passed on June 16, 1933, the last day of the Hundred Days, was viewed as the cornerstone of the recovery program. It sought to stabilize the economy by preventing extreme competition, labor-management conflicts, and over-production. A board composed of industrial and labor leaders in each industry or business drew up a code for that industry which set minimum prices, minimum wages, maximum work hours, production limits, and quotas. The antitrust laws were temporarily suspended. The approach was based on the idea of many economists at the time that a mature industrial economy produced more goods than could be consumed, and that it would be necessary to create a relative shortage of goods in order to raise prices and restore prosperity. The idea was proved wrong by the expansion of consumer goods after World War II. Section 7a of the law also provided that workers had the right to join unions and to bargain collectively. The National Recovery Administration (NRA) was created under the leadership of Hugh

S. Johnson to enforce the law and generate public enthusiasm for it. In May 1935 the law was declared unconstitutional in the case of *Schechter v. United States*, on the grounds that Congress had delegated legislative authority to the code-makers, and that Schechter, who slaughtered chickens in New York, was not engaged in interstate commerce. It was argued later that the NRA had unintentionally aided big firms to the detriment of smaller ones because the representatives of the larger firms tended to dominate the code-making process. It was generally unsuccessful in stabilizing small businesses such as retail stores, and was on the point of collapse when it was declared unconstitutional.

8.2.9 *The Tennessee Valley Authority*

Different from the other legislation of the Hundred Days which addressed immediate problems of the depression, the TVA, a public corporation under a three-member board, was proposed by Roosevelt as the first major experiment in regional public planning. Starting from the nucleus of the government's Muscle Shoals property on the Tennessee River, the TVA built twenty dams in an area of 40,000 square miles to stop flooding and soil erosion, improve navigation, and generate hydroelectric power. It also manufactured nitrates for fertilizer, conducted demonstration projects for farmers, engaged in reforestation, and attempted to rehabilitate the whole area. It was fought unsuccessfully in the courts by private power companies. Roosevelt believed that it would serve as a yardstick to measure the true cost of providing electric power.

8.2.10 *Effects of the First New Deal*

The economy improved but did not get well between 1933 and 1935. The gross national product rose from $74.2 billion in 1933 to $91.4 billion in 1935. Manufacturing salaries and wages increased from $6.24 billion in 1933 to over $9.5 billion in

1935, with average weekly earnings going from $16.73 to $20.13. Farm income rose from $1.9 billion in 1933 to $4.6 billion in 1935. The money supply, as currency and demand deposits, grew from $19.2 billion to $25.2 billion. Unemployment dropped from about 25 percent of nonfarm workers in 1933 to about 20.1 percent, or 10.6 million, in 1935. While the figure had improved, it was a long way from the 3.2 percent of pre-depression 1929, and suffering as a result of unemployment was still a major problem.

CHAPTER 9

THE SECOND NEW DEAL

9.1 OPPOSITION FROM THE RIGHT AND LEFT

9.1.1 *Criticism of the New Deal*

The partial economic recovery brought about by the first New Deal provoked criticism from the right for doing too much, and from the left for doing too little. Conservatives and businessmen criticized the deficit financing, which accounted for about half of the federal budget, federal spending for relief, and government regulation of business. They frequently charged that the New Deal was socialist or communist in form, and some conservative writers labeled the wealthy Roosevelt "a traitor to his class." People on the lower end of the economic scale thought that the New Deal, especially the NRA, was too favorable to big business. Small business people and union members complained that the NRA codes gave control of industry to the big firms, while farmers complained that the NRA set prices too high. The elderly thought that nothing had been done to help them. Several million people who were or had been tenant farmers or sharecroppers were badly hurt. When the AAA paid farmers to take land out of production, the land-owners took the money while the tenants and sharecroppers lost their livelihood. Several opposition organizations and persons were particularly active in opposing Roosevelt's policies:

1) The *American Liberty League* was formed in 1934 by conservatives to defend business interests and promote the open shop. While many of its members were Republicans and it was financed primarily by the Du Pont family, it also attracted conservative Democrats like Alfred E. Smith and John W. Davis. It supported conservative congressional candidates of both parties in the election of 1934 with little success.

2) The *Old Age Revolving Pension Plan* was advanced by Dr. Francis E. Townsend, a retired California physician. The plan proposed that every retired person over sixty receive a pension of $200 a month, about double the average worker's salary, with the requirement that the money be spent within the month. The plan would be funded by a national gross sales tax. Townsend claimed that it would end the depression by putting money into circulation, but economists thought it fiscally impossible. Some three to five million older Americans joined Townsend Clubs.

3) The *Share Our Wealth Society* was founded in 1934 by Senator Huey "The Kingfish" Long of Louisiana. Long was a populist demagogue who was elected governor of Louisiana in 1928, established a practical dictatorship over the state, and moved to the United States Senate in 1930. He supported Roosevelt in 1932, but then broke with him, calling him a tool of Wall Street for not doing more to combat the depression. Long called for the confiscation of all fortunes over five million

dollars and a tax of one hundred percent on annual incomes over one million. With the money the government would provide subsidies so that every family would have a "homestead" of house, car, and furnishings worth at least $5,000, a minimum annual income of $2,000, and free college education for those who wanted it. His slogan was "Every Man a King." Long talked of running for president in 1936, and published a book entitled *My First Days in the White House*. His society had over five million members when he was assassinated on the steps of the Louisiana Capitol on September 8, 1935. The Reverend Gerald L.K. Smith appointed himself Long's successor as head of the society, but he lacked Long's ability.

4) The *National Union for Social Justice* was headed by Father Charles E. Coughlin, a Catholic priest in Royal Oak, Michigan, who had a weekly radio program. Beginning as a religious broadcast in 1926, Coughlin turned to politics and finance, and attracted an audience of millions of many faiths. He supported Roosevelt in 1932, but then turned against him. He advocated an inflationary currency and was anti-Semitic, but beyond that his fascist-like program was not clearly defined.

9.2   THE SECOND NEW DEAL BEGINS

9.2.1   *Roosevelt's Position*

With millions of Democratic voters under the sway of Townsend, Long, and Coughlin, with the destruction of the NRA by the Supreme Court imminent, and with the election of 1936 approaching the next year, Roosevelt began to push through a series of new programs in the spring of 1935. Much of the legislation was passed during the summer of 1935, a period sometimes called the Second Hundred Days.

9.2.2 *Legislation and Programs of the Second New Deal*

The *Works Progress Administration (WPA)* was started in May 1935 following the passage of the Emergency Relief Appropriations Act of April 1935. Headed by Harry Hopkins, the WPA employed people from the relief rolls for thirty hours of work a week at pay double the relief payment but less than private employment. There was not enough money to hire all of the unemployed, and the numbers varied from time to time, but an average of 2.1 million people per month were employed. By the end of the program in 1941, 8.5 million people had worked at some time for the WPA at a total cost of $11.4 billion. Most of the projects undertaken were in construction. The WPA built hundreds of thousands of miles of streets and roads, and thousands of schools, hospitals, parks, airports, playgrounds, and other facilities. Hand work was emphasized so that the money would go for pay rather than equipment, provoking much criticism for inefficiency. Unemployed artists painted murals in public buildings; actors, musicians, and dancers performed in poor neighborhoods; and writers compiled guide books and local histories.

The *National Youth Administration (NYA)* was established as part of the WPA in June 1935 to provide part-time jobs for high school and college students to enable them to stay in school, and to help young adults not in school to find jobs.

The *Rural Electrification Administration (REA)* was created in May 1935 to provide loans and WPA labor to electric cooperatives to build lines into rural areas not served by private companies.

The *Resettlement Administration (RA)* was created in the Agriculture Department in May 1935 under Rexford

Tugwell. It relocated destitute families from seemingly hopeless situations to new rural homestead communities or to suburban greenbelt towns.

The *National Labor Relations* or *Wagner Act* was passed in May 1935 to replace the provisions of Section 7a of the NIRA. It reaffirmed labor's right to unionize, prohibited unfair labor practices, and created the National Labor Relations Board (NLRB) to oversee and insure fairness in labor-management relations.

The *Social Security Act* was passed in August 1935. It established a retirement plan for persons over age sixty-five funded by a tax on wages paid equally by employee and employer. The first benefits, ranging from $10 to $85 per month, were paid in 1942. Another provision of the act had the effect of forcing the states to initiate unemployment insurance programs. It imposed a payroll tax on employers which went to the state if it had an insurance program, and to the federal government if it did not. The act also provided matching funds to the states for aid to the blind, handicapped, and dependent children, and for public health services. The American Social Security system was limited compared with those of other industrialized nations, and millions of workers were not covered by it. Nonetheless, it marked a major change in American policy.

The *Banking Act of 1935* created a strong central Board of Governors of the Federal Reserve System with broad powers over the operations of the regional banks.

The *Public Utility Holding Company* or *Wheeler-Rayburn Act* of 1935 empowered the Securities and Exchange Commission to restrict public utility holding companies to one natural region and to eliminate duplicate holding companies. The Federal Power Commission was created to regulate interstate electrical power rates and activities, and the Federal Trade Commission received the same kind of power over the natural gas companies.

The *Revenue Act* of 1935 increased income taxes on higher incomes, and also inheritance, large gift, and capital gains taxes.

The *Motor Carrier Act* of 1935 extended the regulatory authority of the Interstate Commerce Commission to cover interstate trucking lines.

9.3 THE ELECTION OF 1936

9.3.1 *The Democrats*

At the convention in Philadelphia in June, Roosevelt and Garner were renominated by acclamation on the first ballot. The convention also ended the requirement for a two-thirds vote for nomination. The platform promised an expanded farm program, labor legislation, more rural electrification and public housing, and enforcement of the antitrust laws. In his acceptance speech Roosevelt declared that "this generation of Americans has a rendezvous with destiny." He further proclaimed that he and the American people were fighting for democracy and capitalism against the "economic royalists," business people he charged with seeking only their own power and wealth, and opposing the New Deal.

9.3.2 *The Republicans*

Governor Alfred M. Landon of Kansas, a former progressive supporter of Theodore Roosevelt, was nominated on the first ballot at the convention in Cleveland in June. Frank Knox, a Chicago newspaper publisher, was chosen as his running mate. The platform criticized the New Deal for operating under unconstitutional laws, and called for a balanced budget, higher tariffs, and lower corporate taxes. It did not call for the repeal of all New Deal legislation, and promised better and less expensive relief, farm, and labor programs. In effect, Landon and the Republicans were saying that they would do about the same thing, but do it better.

9.3.3 The Union Party

Dr. Francis Townsend, Father Charles Coughlin, and the Reverend Gerald L.K. Smith, Long's successor in the Share Our Wealth Society, organized the Union Party to oppose Roosevelt. The nominee was Congressman William Lemke of North Dakota, an advocate of radical farm legislation but a bland campaigner. Vicious attacks by Smith and Coughlin on Roosevelt brought a backlash against them, and American Catholic leaders denounced Coughlin.

9.3.4 The Election

Roosevelt carried all of the states except Maine and Vermont with 27,757,333 votes, or 60.8 percent of the total, and 523 electoral votes. Landon received 16,684,231 votes and 8 electoral votes. Lemke had 891,858 votes for 1.9 percent of the total. Norman Thomas, the Socialist candidate, received 187,000 votes, only 21 percent of the 881,951 votes he received in 1932.

9.3.5 The New Deal Coalition

Roosevelt had put together a coalition of followers who made the Democratic party the majority party in the nation for the first time since the Civil War. While retaining the Democratic base in the Solid South and among white ethnics in the big cities, Roosevelt also received strong support from midwestern farmers. Two groups which made a dramatic shift into the Democratic ranks were union workers and blacks. Unions took an active political role for the first time since 1924, providing both campaign funds and votes. Blacks had traditionally been Republican since emancipation, but by 1936 about three-fourths of the black voters, who lived mainly in the northern cities, had shifted into the Democratic party.

9.4   THE LAST YEARS OF THE NEW DEAL

9.4.1   *Court Packing*

Frustrated by a conservative Supreme Court which had overturned much of his New Deal legislation, Roosevelt, after receiving his overwhelming mandate in the election of 1936, decided to curb the power of the court. In doing so, he overestimated his own political power and underestimated the force of tradition. In February 1937 he proposed to Congress the Judicial Reorganization Bill which would allow the president to name a new federal judge for each judge who did not retire by the age of 70 1/2. The appointments would be limited to a maximum of fifty, with no more than six added to the Supreme Court. At the time, six justices were over the proposed age limit. Roosevelt cited a slowing of the judicial process due to the infirmity of the incumbents, and the need for a modern outlook. The president was astonished by the wave of opposition from Democrats and Republicans alike, and uncharacteristically refused to compromise. In doing so, he not only lost the bill but he lost control of the Democratic Congress which he had dominated since 1933. Nonetheless, the Court changed its position as Chief Justice Charles Evans Hughes and Justice Owen Roberts began to vote with the more liberal members. The National Labor Relations Act was upheld in March 1937, and the Social Security Act in April. In June a conservative justice retired, and Roosevelt had the opportunity to make an appointment.

9.4.2 The Recession of 1937-1938

Most economic indicators rose sharply between 1935 and 1937. The gross national product had recovered to the 1930 level, and unemployment, if WPA workers were considered employed, had fallen to 9.2 percent. Average yearly earnings of the employed had risen from $1,195 in 1935 to $1,341 in 1937, and average hourly manufacturing earnings from 55 cents to 62 cents. During the same period there were huge federal deficits. In fiscal 1936, for example, there was a deficit of $4.4 billion in a budget of $8.5 billion. Roosevelt decided that the recovery was sufficient to warrant a reduction in relief programs and a move toward a balanced budget. The budget for fiscal 1938, from July 1937 to June 1938, was reduced to $6.8 billion, with the WPA experiencing the largest cut. During the winter of 1937-1938 the economy slipped rapidly and unemployment rose to 12.5 percent. In April 1938 Roosevelt requested and received from Congress an emergency appropriation of about $3 billion for the WPA, as well as increases for public works and other programs. In July 1938 the economy began to recover, and it regained the 1937 levels in 1939.

9.4.3 Legislation of the Late New Deal

With the threat of adverse Supreme Court rulings removed, Roosevelt rounded out his program during the late thirties:

1) *The Bankhead-Jones Farm Tenancy Act,* passed in July 1937, created the Farm Security Administration (FSA) to replace the Resettlement Administration. The FSA continued the homestead projects, and loaned money to farmers to purchase farms, lease land, and buy equipment. It also set up camps for migrant work-

ers and established rural health care programs.

2) The *National Housing* or *Wagner-Steagall Act,* passed in September 1937, established the United States Housing Authority (USHA) which could borrow money to lend to local agencies for public housing projects. By 1941 it had loaned $750 million for 511 projects.

3) The *Second Agricultural Adjustment Act* of February 1938 appropriated funds for soil conservation payments to farmers who would remove land from production. The law also empowered the Agriculture Department to impose market quotas to prevent surpluses in cotton, wheat, corn, tobacco, and rice if two-thirds of the farmers producing that commodity agreed.

4) The *Fair Labor Standards Act,* popularly called the minimum wage law, was passed in June 1938. It provided for a minimum wage of 25 cents an hour which would gradually rise to 40 cents, and a gradual reduction to a work week of 40 hours, with time and a half for overtime. Workers in small businesses and in public and nonprofit employment were not covered. The law also prohibited the shipment in interstate commerce of manufactured goods on which children under 16 worked.

CHAPTER 10

SOCIAL DIMENSIONS OF THE NEW DEAL ERA

10.1 MINORITIES AND WOMEN

10.1.1 *Blacks and the New Deal*

Blacks suffered more than other people from the depression. Unemployment rates were much higher than for the general population, and before 1933 they were often excluded from state and local relief efforts. Blacks did benefit from many New Deal relief programs, but about forty percent of black workers were sharecroppers or tenants who suffered from the provisions of the first Agricultural Adjustment Act. Roosevelt seems to have given little thought to the special problems of black people, and he was afraid to endorse legislation such as an anti-lynching bill for fear of alienating the southern wing of the Democratic party. Eleanor Roosevelt and Harold Ickes strongly supported civil rights, and a "Black Cabinet" of advisors was assembled in the Interior Department. More blacks were appointed to government positions by Roosevelt than ever before, but the number was still small. When government military contracts began to flow in 1941, A. Philip Randolph, the president of the Brotherhood of Sleeping Car Porters, proposed a black march on Washington to demand equal access to defense jobs. To forestall such an action, Roosevelt issued an executive order on June 25, 1941 establishing the Fair Employment Practices Committee to insure consideration for minorities in defense employment.

10.1.2 *Native Americans and the New Deal*

John Collier, the commissioner of the Bureau of Indian Affairs, persuaded Congress to repeal the Dawes Act of 1887 by passing the Indian Reorganization Act of 1934. The law restored tribal ownership of lands, recognized tribal constitutions and government, and provided loans to tribes for economic development. Collier also secured the creation of the Indian Emergency Conservation Program, an Indian CCC for projects on the reservations. In addition, he helped Indians secure entry into the WPA, NYA, and other programs.

10.1.3 *Mexican-Americans and the New Deal*

Mexican-Americans benefitted the least from the New Deal, for few programs covered them. Farm owners turned against them as farm workers after they attempted to form a union between 1933 and 1936. By 1940 most had been replaced by whites dispossessed by the depression. Many returned to Mexico, and the Mexican-American population dropped almost forty percent from 1930 to 1940.

10.1.4 *Women During the New Deal*

The burden of the depression fell on women as much or more as it did on men. Wives and mothers found themselves responsible for stretching meager budgets by preparing inexpensive meals, patching old clothing, and the like. "Making do" became a slogan of the period. In addition, more women had to supplement or provide the family income by going to work. In 1930 there were 10.5 million working women comprising 29 percent of the work force. By 1940 the figures had grown to over 13 million and 35 percent. There was much criticism of working women based on the idea that they deprived men of jobs. Male job losses were greatest in heavy industry such as factories and mills, while areas of female employment such as retail sales were not hit as hard. Unemployed men seldom sought jobs in the traditional women's fields.

10.2 LABOR UNIONS

10.2.1 *Unions During the First New Deal*

Labor unions had lost members and influence during the twenties, and slipped further during the economic decline of 1929 to 1933. The National Industrial Recovery Act gave them new hope when Section 7a guaranteed the right to unionize, and during 1933 about 1.5 million new members joined unions. It soon became clear that enforcement of the industrial codes by the NRA was ineffective, and labor leaders began to call it the "National Run Around." As a result in 1934 there were many strikes, sometimes violent, including a general strike in San Francisco involving about 125,000 workers.

10.2.2 *Craft versus Industrial Unions*

The passage of the National Labor Relations or Wagner Act in 1935 resulted in a massive growth of union membership, but only at the expense of bitter conflict within the labor movement. The American Federation of Labor was made up primarily of craft unions. Some leaders, especially John L. Lewis, the dynamic president of the United Mine Workers, wanted to unionize the mass production industries, such as automobiles and

UNION GROWTH, 1936 – 1941
(in thousands)

Year	Total Membership	AFL	CIO	Unaffiliated
1936	4,107	3,516	--	591
1937	5,780	3,180	1,991	609
1938	6,081	3,547	1,958	575
1939	6,556	3,878	1,838	840
1940	7,282	4,343	2,154	785
1941	8,698	5,179	2,654	865

rubber, with industrial unions. In 1934 the AFL convention authorized such unions, but the older unions continued to try to organize workers in those industries by crafts. In November 1935 Lewis and others established the Committee for Industrial Organization to unionize basic industries, presumably within the AFL. President William Green of the AFL ordered the CIO to disband in January 1936. When the rebels refused, they were expelled by the AFL executive council in March 1937. The insurgents then reorganized the CIO as the independent Congress of Industrial Organizations to be composed of industrial unions.

10.2.3 The Growth of the CIO

During its organizational period the CIO sought to initiate several industrial unions, particularly in the steel, auto, rubber, and radio industries. In late 1936 and early 1937 it used a tactic called the sit-down strike, with the strikers occupying the workplace to prevent any production. There were 477 sit-down strikes involving about 400,000 workers. The largest was in the General Motors plant in Flint, Michigan, as the union sought recognition by that firm. In February 1937 General Motors recognized the United Auto Workers as the bargaining agent for its 400,000 workers. When the CIO established its independence in March 1937, it already had 1.8 million members, and it reached a membership of 3.75 million six months later.

AFL had about 3.2 million members at that time. By the end of 1941 the CIO had about 2.6 million members, the AFL about 5.2 million, and other unions about 865,000. Union members comprised about 11.5 percent of the work force in 1933, and 28.2 percent in 1941.

10.3 CULTURAL TRENDS OF THE THIRTIES

10.3.1 *Literary Developments*

The writers and intellectuals who had expressed disdain for the middle class materialism of the twenties found it even more difficult to deal with the meaning of the crushing poverty in America and the rise of fascism in Europe during the thirties. Some turned to communism, including the fifty-three writers who signed an open letter endorsing the Communist presidential candidate in 1932. Some turned to proletarian novels, such as Jack Conroy in *The Disinherited* (1933) and Robert Cantwell in *The Land of Plenty* (1934). Ernest Hemingway seemed to have lost his direction in *Winner Take All* (1933) and *The Green Hills of Africa* (1935), but in *To Have and Have Not* (1937), a strike novel, he turned to social realism, and *For Whom the Bell Tolls* (1940) expressed his concern about fascism. Sinclair Lewis also dealt with fascism in *It Can't Happen Here* (1935), but did not show the power of his works of the twenties. John Dos Passos depicted what he saw as the disintegration of American life from 1900 to 1929 in his trilogy *U.S.A.* (1930-1936). William Faulkner sought values in southern life in *Light in August* (1932), *Absalom! Absalom!* (1936), and *The Unvanquished* (1938). The endurance of the human spirit and personal survival were depicted in James T. Farrell's trilogy *Studs Lonigan* (1936) about the struggles of lower-middle-class Irish Catholics in Chicago, Erskine Caldwell's *Tobacco Road* (1932) about impoverished Georgia sharecroppers, and John Steinbeck's *The Grapes of Wrath* (1939) about "Oakies" migrating from the dust bowl to California in the midst of the depression.

10.3.2 *Popular Culture*

The depression greatly reduced the amount of money available for recreation and entertainment. There was an increase in games and sports among family groups and friends. The WPA and the CCC constructed thousands of playgrounds, playing fields, picnic areas, and the like for public use. Roosevelt and Harry Hopkins, the director of the WPA, hoped to develop a mass appreciation of culture through the WPA murals in public buildings, with traveling plays, concerts, and exhibits, and with community arts centers. Beyond some revival of handicrafts, it is doubtful that the program had much effect. There were, however, several popular forms of entertainment:

1) Radio was the favorite form of daily entertainment during the depression because, after the initial cost of the instrument, it was free. There were about forty million radios in the United States by 1938. It provided comedy and mystery shows, music, sports and news. A study at the time indicated that radio tended to make Americans more uniform in their attitudes, taste, speech, and humor.

2) While radio was the form of entertainment most used, the movies were the most popular. By 1939 about sixty-five percent of the people went to the movies at least once a week. The movie industry was one of the few which did not suffer financially from the depression. Movies were the great means of escape, providing release from the pressures of the depression by transporting people to a make-believe world of beauty, mystery, or excitement. Spectacular musicals with dozens of dancers and singers, such as *Broadway Melody of 1936*, were popular. The dance team of Fred Astaire and Ginger

Rogers thrilled millions in *Flying Down to Rio* and *Shall We Dance?* Shirley Temple charmed the public as their favorite child star. Judy Garland rose to stardom in *The Wizard of Oz*, while animated films like *Snow White* appealed to children of all ages. People enjoyed the triumph of justice and decency in *Mr. Smith Goes to Washington* and *You Can't Take It With You* with Jimmy Stewart. Dozens of light comedies starred such favorites as Cary Grant, Katharine Hepburn, Clark Gable, and Rosalind Russell, while Errol Flynn played in such larger-than-life roles as *Robin Hood*. A different kind of escape was found in gangster movies with Edward G. Robinson, James Cagney, or George Raft. Near the end of the decade *Gone With the Wind,* released in 1939 starring Clark Gable and Vivien Leigh, became a timeless classic, while *The Grapes of Wrath* in 1940 commented on the depression itself.

3) The popular music of the decade was swing, and the big bands of Duke Ellington, Benny Goodman, Glenn Miller, Tommy Dorsey, and Harry James vied for public favor. The leading popular singer was Bing Crosby. City blacks refined the country blues to city blues, and interracial audiences enjoyed both city blues and jazz. Black musicians were increasingly accepted by white audiences.

4) Comic strips existed before the thirties, but they became a standard newspaper feature as well as a source of comic books during the decade. "Dick Tracy" began his war on crime in 1931, and was assisted by "Superman" after 1938. "Tarzan" began to swing through the cartoon jungles in 1929, and "Buck Rogers" began the exploration of space in 1930.

CHAPTER 11

NEW DEAL DIPLOMACY AND THE ROAD TO WAR

11.1 EARLY NEW DEAL FOREIGN POLICY

11.1.1 *The Good Neighbor Policy*

Roosevelt and Secretary of State Cordell Hull continued the policies of their predecessors in endeavoring to improve relations with Latin American nations, and formalized their position by calling it the Good Neighbor Policy.

Nonintervention. At the Montevideo Conference of American Nations in December 1933 the United States renounced the right of intervention in the internal affairs of Latin American countries. In 1936 in the Buenos Aires Convention the United States further agreed to submit all American disputes to arbitration. Accordingly, the marines were removed from Haiti, Nicaragua, and the Dominican Republic by 1934. The Haitian protectorate treaty was allowed to expire in 1936, the right of intervention in Panama was ended by treaty in 1936, and the receivership of the finances of the Dominican Republic ended in 1941.

Cuba. The United States did not intervene in the Cuban revolution in the spring of 1933, but it did back a coup by Fulgentio Batista to overthrow the liberal regime of Ramon Grau San Martin in 1934. Batista was given a favorable sugar import status for Cuba in return for establishing a conservative administration. In May 1934 the United States abrogated its Platt Amendment rights in Cuba except for control of the Guantanamo Naval Base.

Mexico. The government of Lazaro Cardenas began to expropriate American property, including oil holdings, in 1934. Despite calls for intervention, Roosevelt insisted only on compensation. A joint commission worked out a settlement which was formally concluded on November 19, 1941.

11.1.2 *The London Economic Conference*

An international conference in London in June 1933 tried to obtain tariff reduction and currency stabilization for the industrialized nations. Roosevelt would not agree to peg the value of the dollar to other currencies because he feared that it might impede his recovery efforts. The conference failed for lack of American cooperation.

11.1.3 *Recognition of Russia*

The United States had not had diplomatic relations with the Union of Soviet Socialist Republics since it was established after the 1917 revolution. In an effort to open trade with Russia, mutual recognition was negotiated in November 1933. The financial results were disappointing.

11.1.4 *Philippine Independence*

The Tydings-McDuffie Act of March 1934 forced the Philippines to become independent on July 4, 1946, rather than grant dominion status which the Filipinos had requested.

11.1.5 *The Reciprocal Trade Agreement Act*

This law, the idea of Cordell Hull, was passed in June 1934. It allowed the president to negotiate agreements which could vary from the rates of the Hawley-Smoot Tariff up to fifty percent. By 1936 lower rates had been negotiated with thirteen nations, and by 1941 almost two-thirds of all American foreign trade was covered by agreements.

11.2 UNITED STATES NEUTRALITY LEGISLATION

11.2.1 *Isolationism*

Belief that the United States should stay out of foreign wars and problems began in the twenties and grew in the thirties. It was fed by House and Senate investigations of arms traffic and the munitions industry in 1933 and 1934, especially an examination of profiteering by bankers and munitions makers in drawing the United States into World War I by Senator Gerald Nye of North Dakota. Books of revisionist history which asserted that Germany had not been responsible for World War I and that the United States had been misled were also influential during the thirties. A Gallup poll in April 1937 showed that almost two-thirds of those responding thought that American entry into World War I had been a mistake. Such feelings were strongest in the Midwest and among Republicans, but were found in all areas and across the political spectrum. Leading isolationists included Congressman Hamilton Fish of New York,

Senator William Borah of Idaho, and Senator George Norris of Nebraska, all Republicans. Pacifist movements, such as the Fellowship of Christian Reconciliation, were influential among college and high school students and the clergy.

11.2.2 *The Johnson Act of 1934*

When European nations stopped payment on World War I debts to the United States, this law prohibited any nation in default from selling securities to any American citizen or corporation.

11.2.3 *The Neutrality Acts of 1935*

Isolationist sentiment prompted Senator Key Pittman, a Nevada Democrat, to propose these laws. Roosevelt would have preferred more presidential flexibility, but Congress wanted to avoid flexibility and the mistakes of World War I. The laws provided that, on outbreak of war between foreign nations, all exports of American arms and munitions to them would be embargoed for six months. In addition, American ships were prohibited from carrying arms to any belligerent, and the president was to warn American citizens not to travel on belligerent ships.

11.2.4 *The Neutrality Acts of 1936*

The laws gave the president authority to determine when a state of war existed, and prohibited any loans or credits to belligerents.

11.2.5 *The Neutrality Acts of 1937*

The laws gave the president authority to determine if a civil war was a threat to world peace and covered by the Neutrality Acts, prohibited all arms sales to belligerents, and allowed the cash and carry sale of nonmilitary goods to belligerents.

11.3 THREATS TO WORLD ORDER

11.3.1 *The Manchurian Crisis*

In September 1931 the Japanese army invaded and seized the Chinese province of Manchuria. The action violated the Nine Power Pact and the Kellogg-Briand Pact. When the League of Nations sought consideration of some action against Japan, Hoover refused to consider either economic or military sanctions. The only American action was to refuse recognition of the action or the puppet state of Manchukuo which the Japanese created.

11.3.2 *Ethiopia*

Following a border skirmish between Italian and Ethiopian troops, the Italian army of Fascist dictator Benito Mussolini invaded Ethiopia from neighboring Italian colonies in October 1935. The League of Nations failed to take effective action, the United States looked on, and Ethiopia fell in May 1936.

11.3.3 *Occupation of the Rhineland*

In defiance of the Versailles Treaty, Nazi dictator Adolph Hitler sent his German army into the demilitarized Rhineland in March 1936.

11.3.4 *The Rome-Berlin Axis*

Germany and Italy, under Hitler and Mussolini, formed an alliance called the Rome-Berlin Axis on October 25, 1936.

11.3.5 *The Sino-Japanese War*

The Japanese launched a full-scale invasion of China in July 1937. When Japanese planes sank the American Gunboat *Panay* and three Standard Oil tankers on the Yangtze River in

December 1937, the United States accepted a Japanese apology and damage payments while the American public called for the withdrawal of all American forces from China.

11.3.6 The "Quarantine the Aggressor" Speech

In a speech in Chicago in October 1937 Roosevelt proposed that the democracies unite to quarantine the aggressor nations. When public opinion did not pick up the idea, he did not press the issue.

11.3.7 German Expansion

Hitler brought about a union of Germany and Austria in March 1938, took the German-speaking Sudetenland from Czechoslovakia in September 1938, and occupied the rest of Czechoslovakia in March 1939.

11.3.8 The Invasion of Poland and the Beginning of World War II

On August 24, 1939 Germany signed a nonaggression pact with Russia which contained a secret provision to divide Poland between them. German forces then invaded Poland on September 1, 1939. Britain and France declared war on Germany on September 3 because of their treaties with Poland. By the end of September Poland had been dismembered by Germany and Russia, but the war continued in the west along the French-German border.

11.4 THE AMERICAN RESPONSE TO THE WAR IN EUROPE

11.4.1 Preparedness

Even before the outbreak of World War II, Roosevelt began a preparedness program to improve American defenses. In May

1938 he requested and received a naval construction appropriation of about one billion dollars. In October, Congress provided an additional $300 million for defense, and in January 1939 a regular defense appropriation of $1.3 billion with an added $525 million for equipment, especially airplanes. Defense spending increased after the outbreak of war. In August 1939 Roosevelt created the War Resources Board to develop a plan for industrial mobilization in the event of war. The next month he established the Office of Emergency Management in the White House to centralize mobilization activities.

11.4.2 *The Neutrality Act of 1939*

Roosevelt officially proclaimed the neutrality of the United States on September 5, 1939. He then called Congress into special session on September 21 and urged it to allow the cash-and-carry sale of arms. Despite opposition from isolationists, the Democratic Congress, in a vote that followed party lines, passed a new Neutrality Act in November. It allowed the cash-and-carry sale of arms and short-term loans to belligerents, but forbade American ships to trade with belligerents or Americans to travel on belligerent ships. The new law was helpful to the Allies because they controlled the Atlantic.

11.4.3 *Changing American Attitudes*

Hitler's armies invaded and quickly conquered Denmark and Norway in April 1940. In May, German forces swept through the Netherlands, Belgium, Luxembourg, and France. The British were driven from the continent, and France surrendered on June 22. Almost all Americans recognized Germany as a threat. They divided on whether to aid Britain or to concentrate on the defense of America. The Committee to Defend America by Aiding the Allies was formed in May 1940, and the America First Committee, which opposed involvement, was incorporated in September 1940.

11.4.4 *Greenland*

In April 1940 Roosevelt declared that Greenland, a possession of conquered Denmark, was covered by the Monroe Doctrine, and he supplied military assistance to set up a coastal patrol there.

11.4.5 *Defense Mobilization*

In May 1940 Roosevelt appointed a Council of National Defense chaired by William S. Knudson, the president of General Motors, to direct defense production and especially to build fifty thousand planes. The Council was soon awarding defense contracts at the rate of $1.5 billion a month. The Office of Production Management was created to allocate scarce materials, and the Office of Price Administration was established to prevent inflation and protect consumers. In June, Roosevelt made Republicans Henry L. Stimson and Frank Kellogg secretaries of war and navy, partly as an attempt to secure bipartisan support.

11.4.6 *Selective Service*

Congress approved the nation's first peacetime draft, the Selective Service and Training Act, in September 1940. Men 21 to 35 were registered, and many were called for one year of military training.

11.4.7 *Destroyers for Bases*

Roosevelt had determined that to aid Britain in every way possible was the best way to avoid war with Germany. He ordered the army and navy to turn over all available weapons and munitions to private dealers for resale to Britain. In September

1940 he signed an agreement to give Britain fifty American destroyers in return for a ninety-nine-year lease on air and naval bases in British territories in Newfoundland, Bermuda, and the Caribbean.

11.5   THE ELECTION OF 1940

11.5.1   *The Republicans*

Passing over their isolationist front-runners, Senator Robert A. Taft of Ohio and New York attorney Thomas E. Dewey, the Republicans nominated Wendell L. Willkie of Indiana, a dark horse candidate. Willkie was a liberal Republican who had been a Democrat most of his life, and the head of an electric utility holding company which had fought against the TVA. The platform supported a strong defense program, but severely criticized the New Deal domestic policies.

11.5.2   *The Democrats*

Roosevelt did not reveal his intentions regarding a third term, but he neither endorsed another candidate nor discouraged his supporters. When the convention came in July, he sent a message to the Democratic National Committee implying that he would accept the nomination for a third time if it were offered. He was then nominated on the first ballot, breaking a tradition which had existed since the time of Washington. Only with difficulty did Roosevelt's managers persuade the delegates to accept his choice of vice president, Secretary of Agriculture Henry A. Wallace, to succeed Garner. The platform endorsed the foreign and domestic policies of the administration.

11.5.3 *The Campaign*

Willkie's basic agreement with Roosevelt's foreign policy made it difficult for him to campaign. Willkie had a folksy approach which appealed to many voters, but he first attacked Roosevelt for the slowness of the defense program, and then, late in the campaign, called him a warmonger. Roosevelt, who lost the support of many Democrats, including his adviser James Farley, over the third term issue, campaigned very little. When Willkie began to gain on the warmongering issue, Roosevelt declared on October 30 that "your boys are not going to be sent into any foreign wars."

11.5.4 *The Election*

Roosevelt won by a much narrower margin than in 1936, with 27,243,466 votes, 54.7 percent, and 449 electoral votes. Willkie received 22,304,755 votes and 82 electoral votes. Socialist Norman Thomas had 100,264 votes, and Communist Earl Browder received 48,579.

11.6 AMERICAN INVOLVEMENT WITH THE EUROPEAN WAR

11.6.1 *The Lend-Lease Act*

The British were rapidly exhausting their cash reserves with which to buy American goods. In January 1941 Roosevelt proposed that the United States provide supplies to be paid for in goods and services after the war. The Lend-Lease Act was passed by Congress and signed on March 11, 1941, and the first appropriation of $7 billion was provided. In effect, the law changed the United States from a neutral to a nonbelligerent on the Allied side.

11.6.2 *The Patrol of the Western Atlantic*

The Germans stepped up their submarine warfare in the Atlantic to prevent the flow of American supplies to Britain. In April 1941 Roosevelt started the American Neutrality Patrol. The American navy would search out but not attack German submarines in the western half of the Atlantic, and warn British vessels of their location.

11.6.3 *Occupation of Iceland*

American marines occupied Iceland, a Danish possession, in July 1941 to protect it from seizure by Germany. The American navy began to convoy American and Icelandic ships between the United States and Iceland.

11.6.4 *The Atlantic Charter*

On August 9, 1941 Roosevelt and Winston Churchill, the British prime minister, met for the first time on a British battleship off Newfoundland. They issued the Atlantic Charter which described a postwar world based on self-determination for all nations. It also endorsed the principles of freedom of speech and religion and freedom from want and fear, which Roosevelt had proposed as the Four Freedoms earlier that year.

11.6.5 *Aid to Russia*

Germany invaded Russia in June 1941, and in November the United States extended lend-lease assistance to the Russians.

11.6.6 *The Shoot-on-Sight Order*

The American destroyer *Greer* was attacked by a German submarine near Iceland on September 4, 1941. Roosevelt ordered the American military forces to shoot on sight at any

German or Italian vessel in the patrol zone. An undeclared naval war had begun. The American destroyer *Kearny* was attacked by a submarine on October 16, and the destroyer *Reuben James* was sunk on October 30, with 115 lives lost. In November, Congress authorized the arming of merchant ships.

11.7 THE ROAD TO PEARL HARBOR

11.7.1 *A Japanese Empire*

Following their invasion of China in 1937, the Japanese began to speak of the Greater East Asia Co-Prosperity Sphere, a Japanese empire of undefined boundaries in east Asia and the western Pacific. Accordingly, they forced out American and other business interests from occupied China, declaring that the Open Door policy had ended. Roosevelt responded by lending money to China and requesting American aircraft manufacturers not to sell to Japan.

11.7.2 *The Embargo of 1940*

Following the fall of France, a new and more militant Japanese government in July 1940 obtained from the German-controlled Vichy French government the right to build air bases and to station troops in northern French Indochina. The United States, fearing that the step would lead to further expansion, responded in late July by placing an embargo on the export of aviation gasoline, lubricants, and scrap iron and steel to Japan, and by granting an additional loan to China. In December the embargo was extended to include iron ore and pig iron, some chemicals, machine tools, and other products.

11.7.3 *The Tripartite Pact*

Japan joined with Germany and Italy to form the Rome-Berlin-Tokyo Axis on September 27, 1940 when it signed the

Tripartite Pact or Triple Alliance with the other Axis powers.

11.7.4 *The Embargo of 1941*

In July 1941 Japan extracted a new concession from Vichy France by obtaining military control of southern Indochina. Roosevelt reacted by freezing Japanese funds in the United States, closing the Panama Canal to Japan, activating the Philippine militia, and placing an embargo on the export of oil and other vital products to Japan.

11.7.5 *Japanese-American Negotiations*

Negotiations to end the impasse between the United States and Japan were conducted in Washington between Secretary Hull and Japanese Ambassador Kichisaburo Nomura. Hull demanded that Japan withdraw from Indochina and China, promise not to attack any other area in the western Pacific, and withdraw from the Tripartite Pact in return for the reopening of American trade. The Japanese offered to withdraw from Indochina when the Chinese war was satisfactorily settled, to promise no further expansion, and to agree to ignore any obligation under the Tripartite Pact to go to war if the United States entered a defensive war with Germany. Hull refused to compromise.

11.7.6 *A Summit Conference Proposed*

The Japanese proposed in August 1941 that Roosevelt meet personally with the Japanese prime minister, Prince Konoye, in an effort to resolve their differences. Such an action might have strengthened the position of Japanese moderates, but Roosevelt replied in September that he would do so only if Japan agreed to leave China. No meeting was held.

11.7.7 *Final Negotiations*

In October 1941 a new military cabinet headed by General Hideki Tojo took control of Japan. The Japanese secretly decided to make a final effort to negotiate, and to go to war if no solution was found by November 25. A new round of talks followed in Washington, but neither side would make a substantive change in its position, and on November 26, Hull repeated the American demand that the Japanese remove all their forces from China and Indochina immediately. The Japanese gave final approval on December 1 for an attack on the United States.

11.7.8 *Japanese Attack Plans*

The Japanese planned a major offensive to take the Dutch East Indies, Malaya, and the Philippines in order to obtain the oil, metals, and other raw materials which they needed. At the same time they would attack Pearl Harbor in Hawaii to destroy the American Pacific fleet to keep it from interfering with their plans.

11.7.9 *American Awareness of Japanese Plans*

The United States had broken the Japanese diplomatic codes, and knew that trouble was imminent. Between December 1 and December 6, 1941, it became clear to administration leaders that Japanese task forces were being ordered into battle. American commanders in the Pacific were warned of possible aggressive action there, but not forcefully. Apparently most American leaders thought that Japan would attack the Dutch East Indies and Malaya, but would avoid American territory so as not to provoke action by the United States. Some argue that Roosevelt wanted to let the Japanese attack so that the American people would be squarely behind the war.

11.7.10 *The Pearl Harbor Attack*

At 7:55 A.M. on Sunday December 7, 1941 the first wave of Japanese carrier-based planes attacked the American fleet in Pearl Harbor. A second wave followed at 8:50 A.M. American defensive action was almost nil, but by the second wave a few antiaircraft batteries were operating and a few army planes from another base in Hawaii engaged the enemy. The United States suffered the loss of two battleships sunk, six damaged and out of action, three cruisers and three destroyers sunk or damaged, and a number of lesser vessels destroyed or damaged. All of the 150 aircraft at Pearl Harbor were destroyed on the ground. Worst of all, 2,323 American servicemen were killed and about 1,100 wounded. The Japanese lost twenty-nine planes, five midget submarines, and one fleet submarine.

11.7.11 *The Declaration of War*

On December 8, 1941 Roosevelt told a joint session of Congress that the day before had been a "date that would live in infamy." Congress declared war on Japan with one dissenting vote. On December 11, Germany and Italy declared war on the United States.

"The ESSENTIALS" of HISTORY

REA's **Essentials of History** series offers a new approach to the study of history that is different from what has been available previously. Compared with conventional history outlines, the **Essentials of History** offer far more detail, with fuller explanations and interpretations of historical events and developments. Compared with voluminous historical tomes and textbooks, the **Essentials of History** offer a far more concise, less ponderous overview of each of the periods they cover.

The **Essentials of History** provide quick access to needed information, and will serve as a handy reference source at all times. The **Essentials of History** are prepared with REA's customary concern for high professional quality and student needs.

UNITED STATES HISTORY

1500 to 1789 From Colony to Republic
1789 to 1841 The Developing Nation
1841 to 1877 Westward Expansion & the Civil War
1877 to 1912 Industrialism, Foreign Expansion & the Progressive Era
1912 to 1941 World War I, the Depression & the New Deal
America since 1941: Emergence as a World Power

WORLD HISTORY

Ancient History (4,500BC to 500AD)
The Emergence of Western Civilization
Medieval History (500 to 1450AD)
The Middle Ages

EUROPEAN HISTORY

1450 to 1648 The Renaissance, Reformation & Wars of Religion
1648 to 1789 Bourbon, Baroque & the Enlightenment
1789 to 1848 Revolution & the New European Order
1848 to 1914 Realism & Materialism
1914 to 1935 World War I & Europe in Crisis
Europe since 1935: From World War II to the Demise of Communism

CANADIAN HISTORY

Pre-Colonization to 1867
The Beginning of a Nation
1867 to Present
The Post-Confederate Nation

If you would like more information about any of these books, complete the coupon below and return it to us or go to your local bookstore.

RESEARCH & EDUCATION ASSOCIATION
61 Ethel Road W. • Piscataway, New Jersey 08854
Phone: (908) 819-8880

Please send me more information about your History Essentials Books

Name _____

Address _____

City _____ State _____ Zip _____